PARADIGMS POWERING CHINA'S RISE
A Historical Perspective

PARADIGMS POWERING CHINA'S RISE
A Historical Perspective

Belal Ehsan Baaquie

Helixtap Technologies, Singapore

 **World Scientific**

EW JERSEY · LONDON · SINGAPORE · BEIJING · SHANGHAI · HONG KONG · TAIPEI · CHENNAI · TOKYO

Published by

World Scientific Publishing Co. Pte. Ltd.
5 Toh Tuck Link, Singapore 596224
USA office: 27 Warren Street, Suite 401-402, Hackensack, NJ 07601
UK office: 57 Shelton Street, Covent Garden, London WC2H 9HE

Library of Congress Cataloging-in-Publication Data
Names: Baaquie, B. E., author.
Title: Paradigms powering China's rise : a historical perspective /
    Belal Ehsan Baaquie, Helixtap Technologies, Singapore.
Description: New Jersey : World Scientific, [2024] | Includes bibliographical references.
Identifiers: LCCN 2023023179 | ISBN 9789811277139 (hardcover) |
    ISBN 9789811277146 (ebook for institutions) | ISBN 9789811277153 (ebook for individuals)
Subjects: LCSH: China--Economic conditions. | Economic development--China--History.
Classification: LCC HC427.5 .B233 2024 | DDC 330.951--dc23/eng/20230630
LC record available at https://lccn.loc.gov/2023023179

British Library Cataloguing-in-Publication Data
A catalogue record for this book is available from the British Library.

Cover design: Kristine Ong

For any available supplementary material, please visit
https://www.worldscientific.com/worldscibooks/10.1142/13433#t=suppl

Desk Editors: Balasubramanian Shanmugam/Pui Yee Lum

Typeset by Stallion Press
Email: enquiries@stallionpress.com

Printed in Singapore

This book is dedicated to my wife Najma Sultana Baaquie and to the rest of our family members for their steadfast and invaluable support over many long years that I have spent in writing this and other books.

Preface

This book focuses on the historical analysis of China's rise and has a companion volume *Contemporary China: Socialist Market Economy and Private Capital* [1] that discusses some of the ideas and events which have arisen due to China's historical rise. The companion volume is recommended for readers who would like to follow up on the contemporary trajectory being followed by China.

The present juncture of the world's development has seen the emergence of a new and powerful China — a China that had been an ancient, sophisticated and advanced civilization for many centuries before experiencing 100 years of setbacks. Its re-emergence has attracted the interest not only of many scholars and social scientists but also of curious minds, since the rise of a country with the size and depth of China is quite unprecedented. This book concentrates on the historical background of China's rise and the innovative paradigms that powered its rise.

My interest in understanding the rise of China goes back many years. During 1969, I was a student at the University of Dhaka that was at the forefront of Bangladesh's maelstrom of national awakening, which culminated in the 1971 Bangladesh War of Liberation. It was in this climate of social turmoil and ferment that I became aware of China, a country that was in the throes of a major upheaval: the Cultural Revolution. My interest in China continued growing while studying and working in the United States and subsequently during my professional life, spent in Southeast Asia dedicated to the fields of theoretical physics and mathematical finance.

My first visit to China was to Beijing in 1987. My second visit was again to Beijing in 2009, my third visit was to Shanghai and Suzhou in 2013, and in 2016, I visited Shenzhen. I was amazed at the rapid modernization of China from Beijing that was full of bicycles in 1987 to what I saw in 2016: revitalized ancient cities — bustling with energy and replete with gleaming ultramodern skyscrapers — connected by high-speed trains and multi-lane highways.

My visits to China reinforced my earlier curiosity of understanding how and why China was able to achieve its rapid rise, especially when compared to other countries of the South.

My academic interest in China was sparked about 20 years ago, in 2003, by discussions with colleagues on applying the techniques of physics to recognize regularities and patterns in history. Our studies showed that Chinese dynasties have exhibited, over the past two millenniums, a cyclical pattern of prolonged periods of unifications and fragmentations [2]. Studies with co-authors on the ancient Silk Road [3] and on the current rivalry between United States and China [4] further increased my interest in studying both ancient and modern China.

The genesis of this book lies in trying to understand the nature of Chinese dynasties. In particular, the factors leading to the founding of a new dynasty and whether it is going to be long-lasting or short-lived. My study of Chinese dynasties led me to study the rise of modern China. Although it is qualitatively different from ancient feudal dynasties, the rise of modern China seems to have some elements of continuity with ancient feudal dynasties, based on certain underlying characteristics of Chinese society.

Debating whether China's rise is illusory or authentic is not the subject of this book, since its emergence as a great power is considered to be a given. The subject of this book is, rather, on understanding the why and how of China's rise. In particular, the main subject of this book is to unpack and analyze the historical background of the underlying paradigms that have powered the rise of modern China.

One of the most significant international dimensions of China's rise is its impact on developing countries. China's rise offers a new perspective for developing countries, providing innovative pathways for their growth and up-liftment. It is important to objectively understand modern China since China provides groundbreaking paradigms for economic partnerships, such as the Belt and Road Initiative. China's rise provides a novel basis for a multipolar and polycentric world and creates options for developing countries to choose between the Global North and China for capital, technology and markets. It is for these and a multitude of other reasons that the groundbreaking paradigms that have powered China's rise are analyzed and dissected.

The rise of China is a vast and complex subject, one that requires as many different perspectives as possible. This book is one such perspective, formed over many decades of observations, by an observer unaffiliated with China and studying modern China from an empirical and quantitative perspective. Therefore, I hope that the readers will view this book from a macro-historical point of view rather than treating it as an academic study of China's rise.

About the Author

Belal Ehsan Baaquie is an advisor to Helix-tap Technologies, Singapore. He was a Professor of Physics at the National University of Singapore (1984–2016) and a Professor of Finance at INCEIF University, Malaysia (2016–2021). Belal Ehsan Baaquie has been trained as a theoretical physicist at Caltech (BS) and Cornell University (PhD), specializing in quantum field theory. He has pioneered the application of quantum mathematics to economics and finance and has written many books and research papers on quantum physics (including quantum computers), finance, economics and mathematics. He has also written books on science and physics for undergraduates. Over the years, he has extended his research interests to Islamic finance, history and politics. He is an editor of the journal *China and the World* and has written many articles on China. His page on Amazon is at https://www.amazon.com/Belal-E-Baaquie/e/B07GCC7WQ4%3 Fref=dbs_a_mng_rwt_scns_share.

Acknowledgments

I would like to acknowledge and express my heartfelt thanks to many colleagues, friends and scholars who have, over many decades, helped to shape my views about China. Discussions with them opened up new vistas for navigating and understanding the rise of China: a challenging and complex world historical event.

I would like to thank Bertrand Roehner for an enjoyable collaboration. I am especially indebted to Wang Qing-hai for many interesting discussions and for his in-depth reading of the manuscript; his wide-ranging knowledge of China and his deep insights have greatly helped to highlight and clarify many important issues.

Contents

Part I
Foreground

Chapter 1

Synopsis

This book is on China's rise, with especial emphasis on the last 100 years, and is a historical summary of how China's rise has been accomplished. It focuses primarily on China's history up to 2019, with special emphasis on the period 1979–2019; references are made to earlier and later years as and when necessary.

Some notation that is used in this book are the following:

- **CPC**: Communist Party of China.
- **PRC**: People's Republic of China.
- **Global North**: This refers primarily to the United States, the United Kingdom, Europe, Japan, South Korea, Canada, Australia, and New Zealand.
- **Global South**: This refers to Asia, Africa and Latin America.
- Quotations and emphasis are in italics.

This book is organized in five parts that have the following components:

I: Foreground

- **Chapter 1**: This chapter covers the synopsis and explains the scope and structure of the book.
- **Chapter 2**: This chapter provides a strategic perspective of China's rise and discusses the method adopted for the exposition in this book.

II: Assessing China's Rise

- **Chapter 3**: This chapter is an empirical study of China's macroeconomy so as to provide a quantitative basis for understanding and defining China's rise.
- **Chapter 4**: This chapter focuses on China's peaceful rise.
- **Chapter 5**: This chapter provides the summary of Part II.

III: Historical Background to China's Rise

- **Chapter 6**: This chapter provides a historical background to China's rise. The history of China is a complex and immense subject, spanning more than 5,000 years. This chapter focuses on the last 2,000 years, since the time of China's first unification in 221 BC.
- **Chapter 7**: The rise of China is inseparably tied to the rise of the CPC. This chapter traces the rise of the Party through many twists and turns; the history of the Party shows its inner workings as well as the important role of the leaders of the Chinese revolution.
- **Chapter 8**: This chapter provides the summary of Part III.

IV: China's State and Economy

- **Chapters 9–11**: These chapters provide a detailed discussion of the various paradigms for development that China has innovated.
- **Chapter 12**: This chapter provides a summary of Part IV.

V: Paradigms and China's Rise

- **Chapter 13**: This chapter summarizes the groundbreaking paradigms that are powering China's rise.
- **Chapter 14**: This chapter provides a conclusion to this book.

Chapter 2

Strategic Perspective

In 2021, China celebrated 100 years of the founding of the Communist Party of China (CPC), and an appropriate occasion to review the progress China has made; in particular to examine China's path of development and its model for economic growth. There are many narratives on China's rise that are mostly based on secondary and tertiary sources. In contrast, this book attempts to use, as far as possible, primary sources to construct an alternative narrative about the rise of the People's Republic of China. The purpose of this alternative narrative is to provide a balanced analysis and deduce the underlying principles and *creative development paradigms* that underpin the governance of China and that led to its rise.

Noteworthy 2.1. Paradigm

The Cambridge English Dictionary defines *paradigm* as a model of something or a very clear and typical example of something. The term *paradigm* is defined to be a set of assumptions, concepts, values, and practices that constitute a way of viewing reality for the community that shares the paradigm. The synonyms of paradigm are model, pattern, example, standard, prototype, archetype, ideal, gauge, criterion, paragon, and exemplar.

(Continued)

Noteworthy 2.1. (*Continued*)

Development paradigms refers to the manner in which a social system is organized for guiding the socio-economic development of the economy and of the country, as well as its relation to the rest of the world.

China is widely acknowledged, far and wide, as a great power, especially since 2019. China's rise has brought 800 million people out of poverty and has provided the world with a powerful engine of growth. The Secretary-General of the United Nations has hailed this achievement in 2019.[1] In discussing the rise of a nation of 1.4 billion people to becoming a great power — a milestone in the history of humankind — an empirical and quantitative approach, based on facts and statistics, makes for a multi-dimensional understanding of China's rise.

The indicators for the rise of China are discussed in some detail in Section 3.10 of Chapter 3. This book analyses the momentous events that took place in the long and complex path taken by a poor and populous peasant society in transforming itself from a semi-colony into a global behemoth and a modern industrial, scientific and technological powerhouse — and that too in a matter of mere seven decades. Instead of concentrating on contemporary issues, historical and social factors are dissected to explain how China could rise from poverty, from being the 'sick man of Asia', and answer the historical question:

How did China accomplish its rise?

Noteworthy 2.2. Comparisons with China's social and political system

No attempt is made to deliberate on China's current social system or to compare it with that of other countries, except for illustrating some key features. A comparative study of China's

(*Continued*)

Noteworthy 2.2. (*Continued*)

system. with other countries has been carried out by many authors [16, 44].

The basis of the political power of the CPC requires an analysis on how power is apportioned in China. How China's leaders are selected and whether this process is better than the one person, one vote system is a complicated subject that needs a detailed discussion in its own right and has been discussed in Refs. [9, 16, 44]. The internal mechanism for the governance of the CPC is addressed in Ref. [44]. The fact that the CPC has been holding state power for over 70 years is analyzed for the consequences that have followed thereof.

2.1 Salient Features of China's Rise

There are two cardinal features of China's rise that this book will illustrate.

1. After exploring and trying many different paths for its social development, based on the China's historical experiences and objective conditions, China chose the pioneering path that led to the founding of the PRC in 1949 under the leadership of the CPC.
2. The innovative paradigms chosen for China's development are groundbreaking and without any historical precedent.

Some of the salient facts about China's rise that are addressed in subsequent chapters are the following:

- China is the first developing country that has transformed itself into a scientific and technological innovator as well as an industrial powerhouse.
- China is a major developing country to reach the status of a moderately prosperous country by 2022, starting from being a semi-feudal and semi-colonial country in 1949.[2]

A forecast, based on China's current macroeconomic trajectory, predicts that by end of 2023 China will have crossed the notorious 'middle nation trap' and become a high-income country.

The only other examples are that of South Korea and Taiwan, both of which modernized their economies by the 1990s under the impetus of US capital and as a part of the Cold War (1945–1991).

- China was a historically a rich and powerful country for many centuries, which had become weak and impoverished. The social, historical and economic foundations of China show that the rise of China is no flash in the pan and it is not a copycat nation playing 'catch-up' with other leading nations, but it is rather the rejuvenation of an ancient civilization.

- China has broken over 2,000 years of feudal bondage and a century of humiliation and domination at the hands of imperialist powers to emerge as a premium nation and a peer competitor of the advanced countries. (The term *feudalism* is used for characterizing the social system of pre-modern China and is further discussed in Section 6.1.1 of Chapter 6.)

- The rise of the PRC is inextricably tied to the rise of the CPC, which has played an indispensable role in leading China's transformation from a semi-feudal and semi-colonial society to a leading nation of the world. (The CPC has characterized pre-1949 China as a semi-feudal and semi-colonial society, which is briefly discussed in Section 7.2 of Chapter 7.)

- China has employed innovative and original paradigms for development and shown new paths to prosperity that are open to all countries of the developing world.

- China's rise has led to it having the heft and strength to engage with other powerful countries as an equal, thus laying the grounds for ending the era of a unipolar world and ushering in the beginnings of a multi-polar and polycentric world.

2.2   Paradigms for Governance

Numerous books, articles and reports have been written on the vast and complex subject of China's rise, with views both supporting and opposing China's rise [5–7, 9–11, 14–18]. The rise of China, by all indicators, is heading towards being the defining event of the

21st century, leading to a shift in the center of gravity of the world from the Global North to East Asia and in general to Eurasia. It is timely that this momentous and far-reaching shift in the geopolitics of the world is analyzed from many different frames of reference and standpoints.

This book analyzes the foundations of China's rise and the historical trajectory followed by China. The social system that the CPC has put in place is studied, with the main focus on explaining China's rapid rise from the vantage point of *development paradigms* of China. The analysis utilizes quantitative indicators for economic and social issues and draws largely upon Chinese sources for economic data.

As mentioned earlier, the narrative on the rise of China is best explained by relying on primary sources regarding China's development paradigms. As far as possible, China's own narrative, with its views of itself and of the world, is constructed from the pronouncements of those who speak for the PRC, including its leaders. In particular, the views expressed by Xi Jinping, the leader of the CPC, are taken to be the authoritative position of the CPC and used to analyze the Party's role in China [19].

The foundations of China's rise rest on the methods adopted by the CPC for choosing the *paradigms* for China's development, including its *planning, policies* and *directions*. One of the main conclusions of this book is that the development paradigms adopted by the CPC — which, with hindsight, have been shown to be by and large effective — have led to the rapid rise of China.

There are two criteria for judging China's rise:

1. **Subjective criterion**: This is based on the goals that the CPC has set for itself. These are discussed in Section 2.3.
2. **Objective criterion**: This is based on an empirical account of China's macroeconomy and comparisons with other countries discussed in Chapter 3.

2.3 Founding Mission of the CPC

The People's Republic of China (PRC) has been governed by the CPC since 1949. The CPC provides comprehensive leadership over almost every aspect of life in China from the government, army, economy and to society at large. The CPC is a political Party and does not directly run the administration of the government. (The relation of the CPC to the governance of China is discussed in Chapter 9.)

In 2021, Xi Jinping stated that the *founding mission* and goals of the CPC to be the following [20]:

Party has made seeking happiness for the Chinese people and rejuvenation for the Chinese nation its aspiration and mission. All the struggle, sacrifice, and creation through which the Party has united and led the Chinese people over the past hundred years has been tied together by one ultimate theme of bringing about the great rejuvenation of the Chinese nation.

The founding spirit of the Party is comprised of the following principles: upholding truth and ideals, staying true to our original aspiration and founding mission, fighting bravely without fear of sacrifice, and remaining loyal to the Party and faithful to the people.

[The Party has made] substantive progress towards achieving well rounded human development and **common prosperity** *for all.*

The fundamental and unchanging objective of the CPC, according to Xi Jinping, is *to realize the Chinese dream*,[3] which is the rejuvenation of the Chinese nation, and has culminated in setting the following centennial goals:

- establishing China as a moderately prosperous society by 2021, the 100 year anniversary of the founding of the CPC;
- transforming China into a great modern socialist country by 2049, the 100th anniversary of the founding of the PRC.

The CPC has also set a more specific set of medium term goals for China. Some of these goals are the following:

- The 'Made in China 2025' is a 10 year national plan designed to turn China from a manufacturing giant into a global high-tech industrial powerhouse.
- China aims to realize socialist modernization by 2035.
- To achieve common prosperity, a theme that has been at the focal point of a relatively recent change of economic direction is discussed in Section 11.2 of Chapter 11.

With this mission in mind, the CPC has set policy guidelines and development goals for China.[4]

2.4 Macroconomic Criteria

To address the question, *How successful has the CPC been in fulfilling its founding mission?*, one needs to analyze the following four foundational pillars on which a country's social development can be taken to be based upon:

1. the competence and dynamism of the political system, in particular the quality of its leadership and the competence of the social and political elites;
2. the organization of its economic system and its technological resources;
3. the weaponry, capabilities and organization of its military and the level of its military technology;
4. the quality of life of the country (determined by personal safety, public utilities, health, education, modern cities and so on), its cultural and social values, in other words the country's 'way of life'.

The economic prosperity of a country is the touchstone of both the competence of the political leadership as well of the technological expertise of the country. All aspects of a country, including its military strength as well as its quality of life, hinge on the country's economic prowess. The economic foundations of a country is a transparent and quantitative gauge for assessing the overall level of a country's development and falls within the field of macroeconomics. Hence, of the four factors that are a gauge of a country's level of development, it is sufficient to focus on point number 2, as it will elucidate the impact of CPC's leadership on China's economic progress.

In Chapter 3, China's macroeconomic system is studied to understand China's rise. A variety of empirical indicators are analyzed to measure the economic and social progress made by the PRC over the last four decades in order to measure how far China has progressed. To assess if the PRC has been relatively more successful than the development of other countries, a variety of comparisons are made in Section 4.3 of Chapter 4.

The CPC's *leadership* role in the PRC, which follows from the fact that state power is wielded by the CPC, is the key to understanding China's governance. The innovations introduced by the CPC in the social organization of the PRC and its system of governance, with particular emphasis on its *economic system*, are reviewed in various chapters. Instead of carrying out a comprehensive analysis of this vast subject, a few points are highlighted to add to the ongoing analysis of China's rise.

Endnotes

[1] https://www.un.org/press/en/2019/sgsm19779.doc.htm.
[2] The modernization of Japan starting from the Meiji restoration in 1868 is quite different from China since Japan was never a developing country and modernized along the same pattern as the colonizing European countries. The same is true of the Russian empire, which was also a colonizing power.
[3] https://www.globaltimes.cn/page/201712/1082792.shtml.
[4] http://www.xinhuanet.com/english/2020-01/07/c_138685784.htm.

Part II
Assessing China's Rise

Chapter 3

China's Macroeconomy

As mentioned in Section 2.4 of Chapter 2, the state of China's macroeconomy is taken to be a touchstone of how far has China progressed since the founding of the PRC. This chapter is primarily an empirical analysis of China's macroeconomy and dissects China's macroeconomy using transparent and publicly accessible data. The fundamental pillars of China's macroeconomy are empirically analyzed and the current state of China's economy is described using a few key indicators, including the yearly gross domestic product (GDP).

3.1 Introduction

The economic rise of China is historically unprecedented — no country has been able to uplift over 800 million out of poverty in the short span of 40 years.[1] The rise is all the more remarkable given that at its starting point in 1949, China's per capita income was lower than many Asian and African countries. For example, in 1952, the per capita GDP of China was $538 compared to $629 for India. In 1978, the per capita GDP of China ($978), almost equal to India ($966), was only one-twentieth of the United States.[2]

In 40 years, from 1978 to 2018, Chinese per capita income increased from 171 yuan to 28,228 yuan, an average increase of over 6.1% increase on a year-by-year basis (inflation-adjusted).[3] In 2020, the yearly per capita income in China was 120,000 yuan (about $14,000). Figures 3.1 and 3.2 show China's rising GDP, with the

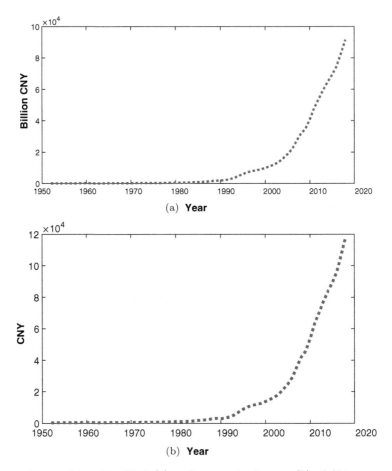

Figure 3.1. The GDP (a) and per capita income (b) of China.

per capita income and total wages of Chinese workers rising in tandem with the country's GDP.

In terms of dollar valuation, China's GDP was $150 billion in 1978, reaching $1,434 billion by 2019 (see Figure 3.1). In terms of purchasing power parity (PPP), discussed in Section 3.10, China was already the biggest economy in the world by 2017.[4]

Figures 3.1 and 3.2 show that the GDP and per capita income in China have increased dramatically from 1990. As observed by Mahbubani [16], never in the 5,000 years of China's history have such a vast number of Chinese people experienced so much prosperity and

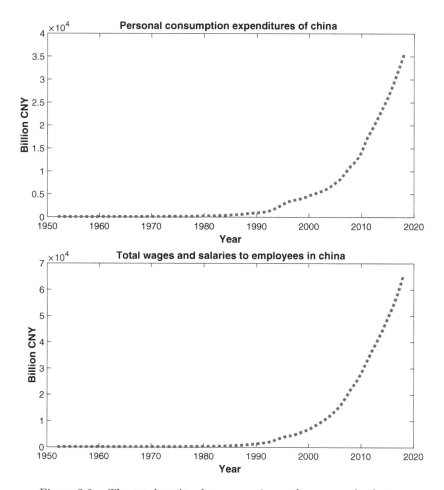

Figure 3.2. The total national consumption and wages and salaries.

that too over such a short period. Figure 3.2 shows that wages sharply increased from 1990 onward, with revenues and profits generated by the expansion of the economy leading to an increase in total salaries and wages.

3.2 Macroeconomic Indicators

Major macroeconomic indicators of China (all data are given per year) reflect the overall state of the economy and provide a clear empirical basis for assessing the economic rise of China.

The following are some key macroeconomic indicators:

- GDP, which is the total value of all the goods and services produced in a country;
- personal consumption;
- government expenditures, including expenditure on infrastructure,
  public education and health, salaries of civil servants, military budget, and so on; the figures are for the cumulative investments made
  from the founding of the PRC to the present year;
- fixed asset investment on new machinery, technology, raw materials, assets such as land, factory buildings and so on; the figures
  are for the cumulative investments made from the founding of the
  PRC to the present year;
- the total number of workers employed;
- total wages of the workers and employees;
- domestic interest rate;
- money supply (M2) that is controlled by the central bank[5];
- international trade (imports, exports, balance of payment).

Other indicators such as taxation, inflation, cost of living, overseas
earnings and foreign exchange rate for its currency are not addressed.

3.3   Investment in Education

After the opening up in 1979, China made large investments in education. The number of kindergartens rose from 1,799 in 1950 to 267,000
in 2018. The enrollment in elementary schools rose from 20% in 1949
to 99.95% in 2018. Higher education enrollment increased from 0.26%
in 1949 to 48.1% in 2018.[6]

There was an increase, from 675 in 1980 to 1,065 in 1993, in
the number of higher education institutions, with student numbers
increasing, by 2.22 times, from 1.14 million in 1980 to 2.54 million in
1993. The number of university students per 10,000 increased from
11.6 in 1980 to 19.9 in 1993. From 1980 to 1993, the government
invested 464.65 billion yuan in education. Education expenditure in
the state's fiscal budget increased from less than 10% in 1980 to over
16% in 1993 [8].

From 1993 to 2003, China doubled the number of colleges and universities to 2,409. Since 1998, China has invested billions of yuan into nine elite Chinese universities to attain world-class status. From 2013 onward, China made a $250 billion-a-year investment in education.[7] China is projected to have a total of nearly 195 million graduates by 2020 compared with 120 million in the United States.[8]

In 2021, 8.3 million students graduated from undergraduate programs at public colleges and universities in China, which was nearly double the number of the United States. Of the 8.3 million Chinese graduates, around 4.3 million earned a bachelor's degree, whereas four million earned a more practically oriented short-cycle degree. Students graduated with about 773,000 master's and doctor's degrees.[9]

3.4 Labor Force and Productivity

The reason that China could *rapidly* develop a vast highly skilled working force is largely due to the following: (a) massive investment in education with emphasis on vocational and technical colleges, and (b) social progress resulting from the first 30 years of the PRC, discussed in Section 10.2 of Chapter 10, with literacy rising to almost 80% by 1978; (c) the legacy of human capital built up during the feudal era, as discussed in Sections 6.5 of Chapter 6.

As shown in Figure 3.2, the total labor force steadily expanded from 1950 and the increase slowed down after 1990. The fact that the number of workers was growing at a rate faster than the GDP for the period 1950–1990 was one of the reasons that an urgent change in the paradigm of the economy was required and which was implemented in 1979.

By 2019, China had a 900-million-strong labor force.[10] The labor force has a vast number of highly skilled workers over a wide range of industries, that include high-precision work using advanced tools in fields such as new materials, digital machine tools, energy-saving and new energy vehicles. It is estimated that, by 2025, the total number of skilled workers required in 10 key areas of China's manufacturing industry will be close to 62 million.[11]

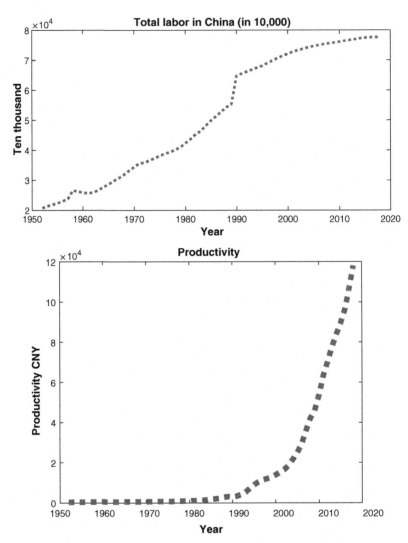

Figure 3.3.   China's total working force and productivity defined as GDP per worker.

Labor productivity is GDP per worker, defined by the total GDP (Y) divided by the total number of workers (L) and is equal to Y/L. China has had a rapid growth in the productivity of its working force, as seen in Figure 3.3. There is a view held by many economists that **the principal and main reason** for the rapid growth of China's economy is due to the spectacular rise in worker's productivity.

3.5 Expansion of Infrastructure

The GDP of China started its rapid rise in 1990, which itself was the result of 10 years of build-up from the reforms of 1979. Fixed assets kept pace with the rapid rise of the GDP; investments in fixed assets and personal consumption followed the steep rise in GDP, as shown in Figure 3.4. The large-scale infrastructure capacity has provided an important foundation for China's industrialization and urbanization.

Over the last 70 years, China has become an infrastructure giant, building highways, airports, bridges, ports and rails and so on. Under the Belt and Road Initiative starting in 2013, China has gone onto to building infrastructure worldwide. The following are a number of infrastructure projects that highlight China's achievements:[12]

- the Three Gorges Dam, the world's biggest hydropower project in terms of electricity production;
- China's South-to-North Water Diversion Project, the biggest water transfer project globally, which benefits 100 million people;
- the world's longest pipelines, including the giant West–East Gas Pipeline project, with a length of 8,704 km;
- the world's highest railway, the Qinghai–Tibet railway, with its highest point reaching an altitude of 5,072 m;
- the world's longest cross-sea bridge, the 55 km-long Hong Kong–Zhuhai–Macao Bridge;
- the world's longest underwater tube tunnel at 6.7 km;
- the world's largest network of high-speed railway, two-thirds of the world's total mileage, which by the end of 2019 was 33,200 km.

By the end of 2018, the total railway operation mileage reached 131,000 km, five times higher than in 1949. Inland waterways expanded 72.7%, to 127,000 km in mileage, while civil aviation flight

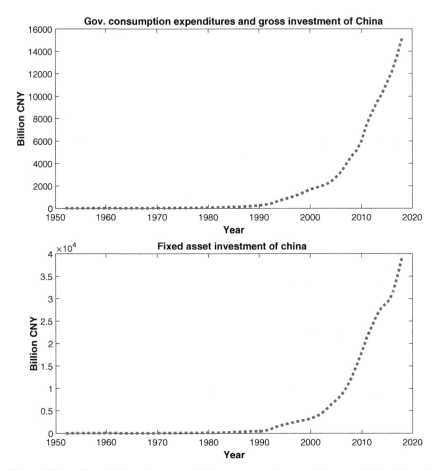

Figure 3.4. Cumulative (not yearly) government expenditure and fixed asset investments.

routes increased to 8.38 million km in 2018, an increase of 734 times from 1950.

Telecom networks expanded rapidly, with the number of postal service branches increasing 9.4 times over the seven decades, reaching 275,000. China's mobile broadband network users were over 1.31 billion in 2018.

3.6 Reforms in Agriculture

Reforms in the countryside, starting in 1978, led to more efficient farming techniques in the newly established small agricultural businesses. Prior to the reforms, in 1979 nearly 80% of China's workforce was working in agriculture; as shown in Figure 3.5, by 1996, this was down to 50% and had fallen to 25% by 2019.[13] Having 25% of the total population living in the rural China has been more or less constant, as has also been the case with highly industrialized South Korea, which has a rural population of 19%.[14]

The rise of efficiency in agricultural production resulted from the 1983 policy of dissolving the People's Communes and replacing it by the Household Responsibility System (HSR), although it had already started since 1978. The government from 1983 onward allowed rural–urban migration, which was previously strictly controlled by the People's Communes, and even encouraged Special Economic Zone set up in Shenzhen to recruit labor from the countryside. HSR led to the freeing of millions of farmers from subsistence farming to higher-value-added manufacturing: this also resulted in a rapid growth of non-agricultural private enterprises. Figure 3.5 shows that the rise in labor productivity mirrors the fall in the number of workers employed in agriculture.[15] China transformed a large population of subsistence

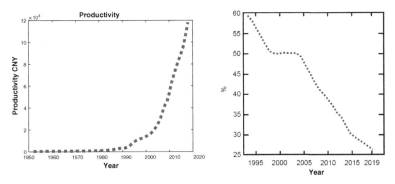

Figure 3.5.   Productivity of labor and the percentage, from 1991 to 2019, of total Chinese workforce employed in agriculture.

farmers into industrial workers, moving 600 million people from countryside to city in less than 40 years — historically the biggest ever rural to urban migration. In doing so, it increased their per capita income 10-fold (from 1992 to 2020)[16] and further fueled the industrialization of China. The change made in agriculture was crucial since, during the 1950s, most of the population was living in rural China.[17]

The strategy of opening up to the world economy was successful due to the transformation of agriculture; without such a transformation, it would not have been possible for China to have a growth rate of 9–10% for many years.

3.6.1 *China's Rural–Urban Migration*

A major cause of the urban migration was in response to the growing labor demand in the cities due to the economic reforms of 1979. The rural-based Township and Village Enterprises (TVEs), discussed in Section 10.6.1 of Chapter 10, were established in 1984. The TVEs were, by and large, the former People's Commune enterprises that were renamed township-owned enterprises and former brigade enterprises that were renamed village-owned enterprises. The TVEs employed 127 million workers by the time they were phased out in 2000.

The HRS and TVEs freed millions of labor force from being tied to agriculture and would later, starting in the 1990s, lead to a massive migration to the cities. Millions of farmers became migrant workers from impoverished rural areas to prosperous urban regions seeking off-farm employment. In 2014, the number of migrant workers had reached 274 million [22].

China's rural population in 2014 was 619 million, accounting for 45% of the total. Agriculture could not absorb the rural working force, especially with increasing productivity in farming. This was the main 'push-factor' forcing urban migration. The other push factor was that weather and other issues result in a high variability and instability of household incomes that makes rural labor to seek additional sources of livelihood.

The main 'pull-factor' for the rural to urban migration was the difference in the income of rural versus urban residents, which was 1:3 in 2014. The two reasons hindering migration was the cost of migration and the lack of information on the urban labor market.

Since 2000, the Chinese government is among a handful of countries that have introduced a series of policies to address the issues arising from rural–urban migration [22].

3.7   International Trade

As seen in Figure 3.6, China's international trade has grown by leaps and bounds, keeping up with the overall growth of the macroeconomy. China has had a growing trade surplus, as seen in Figure 3.6, which rose sharply from 2010 onward, reflecting the growing competitive edge of China in the world market, largely due to its increasingly comprehensive supply chain and large gains in labor productivity. China's massive trade surplus of $419.2 billion with the US in 2018 was the reason given by Donald Trump, the then President of the United States, for the onset of the US trade war with China. He stated: *trade deficits represent an existential threat to US jobs and national security. China makes up the largest part of the US trade deficit.*[18]

3.8   China's Savings and Interest Rates

High interest rates of over 11% prior to 1995 were brought down dramatically to around 5.5% to provide sufficient liquidity for powering the expansion of the economy; see Figure 3.7. A sudden hike of interest rates in 2008 was a response to the 2008 global financial crisis, and interests were finally brought down to less than 4.5% from 2015 onward to sustain high economic growth; see Figure 3.7. Money supply was increased in tandem with the increase in GDP as well as investments made in fixed assets, as can be seen by comparing Figure 3.1 with Figure 3.7.

World Bank data, given in Figure 3.8, shows that China had a consistently high level of domestic savings from 1970 onward.[19] China has the highest global savings rate — higher than than other high-saving East Asian countries — with 32.4% of GDP in 1978 (global average of 23.8%) and 45.4% of GDP in 2017 (the global average of 25.8%).[20] China's private sector savings rate accounted for 92.7% of national savings in 2017, with 45.4% from corporate savings and 47.3% from household savings.[21]

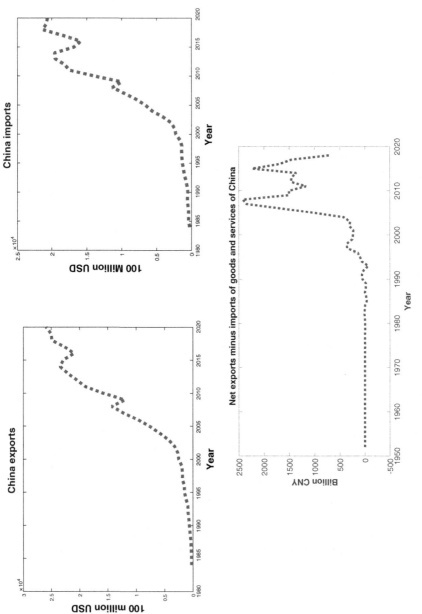

Figure 3.6.   The yearly exports and imports of China at current prices: net exports minus imports of the Chinese economy.

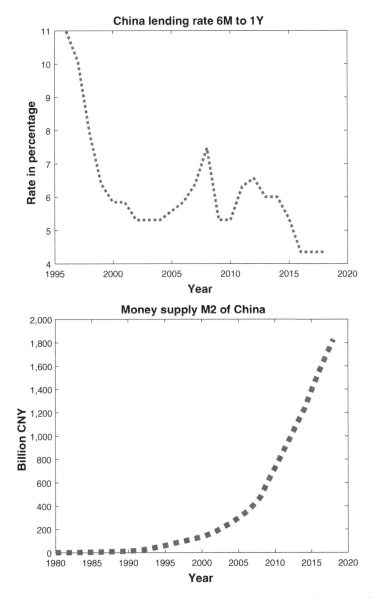

Figure 3.7.   Interest rates (1995–2020) and money supply (1980–2020).

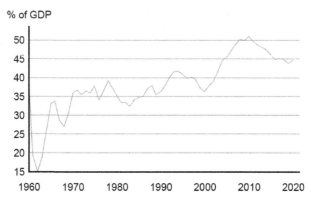

Figure 3.8.   China's gross domestic savings rate.

The high rate of domestic savings provided China with the capital that made possible crucial investments required for the industrialization and modernization of China.

3.8.1   *China's Economic Rise*

China's rise has many dimensions: political, economic, geostrategic, ideological and so on. Underpinning all aspects of China's rise is its economic prowess and dynamism. In summary, the following factors, reinforcing each other, were the main driving forces that powered China's rapid economic growth:

1. Funds at the disposal of the state — based on a high rate of domestic savings as well as fueled by the massive inflow of foreign capital — were used for making large-scale investments in education, constructing a vast infrastructure, and for accumulating capital goods. This led to the growth in the country's stock of fixed assets, such as new factories, manufacturing machinery, the telecommunications systems and so on.
2. Rapid urbanization, which was the result of mass migration of subsistence farmers from the countryside to the city as well as the growth of the urban population, led to the growth in the number of Chinese industrial workers.
3. A rapid and sustained increase in China's labor productivity fueled by a world-class infrastructure, major improvements in the educational level of the working force, the increasing sophistication of capital goods as well as farm workers joining

the industrial workforce. As mentioned earlier, the increase in labor productivity is considered by many analysts as the **most important factor** in the rise of China's economy.

3.9 Technological Innovations

Innovation is widely recognized as being the main driver of technological and economic advancement in the 21st century. China is already a leader in a number of high-tech fields. China's high-speed rail network hit the 40,000-km mark by the end of 2021, reaching 93% of cities with a population of over 500,000; over the past decade, cumulative railway fixed-asset investment has topped $1.05 trillion. China has the world's largest network of high-speed rails, expressways and world-class ports.[22] China has the largest technologically advanced network, with 413 million 5G mobile phone users. China's submersible vessels are leading the world and have reached a depth of 10,000 m. China has developed its own autonomous vehicles, commercial aircraft and launched its own space station.[23]

According to Deng Xiaoping, discussed in Ref. [1], China considers science and technology to be the **primary productive force**, with all major innovations and inventions originating in new ideas in science and technology. For this reason, China has been consistently increasing its investment in research and development (R&D), as shown in Figure 3.9.

China's annual R&D spending grew over 150 times from around $2.21 billion at the beginning of the 1990s to $377 billion in 2020, and further increased to $441.13 billion in 2021. As shown in Figure 3.9, China's R&D:GDP ratio has grown steadily and reached 2.44% in 2021, which is near the 2.47% level of the developed Organisation for Economic Co-operation and Development (OECD) countries.[24] China's total R&D expenditures overtook Japan's in 2013, becoming the world's second after the United States.[25] The scientific literacy of China has increased from 6.2% in 2015 to 10.5% in 2020. China's global ranking in innovation rose from 34 in 2012 to 12 in 2021.[26]

China surpassed the US in terms of the number of academic research papers in 2021; see Figure 3.9. China has been leading the world in the number of new patent filings since 2011. Starting from zero patent applications in 1985, China had 68,720 new filings in 2020; in 2021, Chinese applicants filed 69,540 applications,

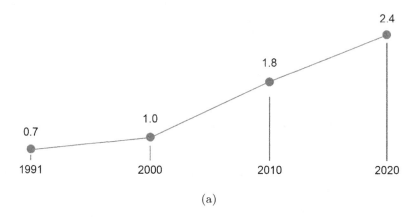

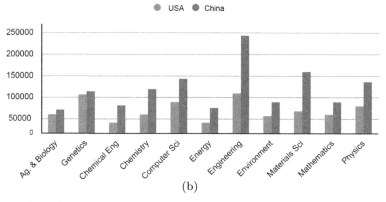

Figure 3.9.   (a) China's research and development expenditure in 2020 and (b) scientific publications of China and the United States in 2021.

compared with 59,570 applications filed by their US counterparts.[27] China had the most patents worldwide in 2019, with a total of 452,804 patents granted to resident and non-resident companies or organizations, followed by the United States with 354,430 granted patents.[28]

China is in competition with the United States for leadership in research and applications of Artificial Intelligence (AI), which is discussed further in Ref. [1]. Automated warehouses, smart ports running on 5G networks, mines operated by remote control, factories run by self-programming robots and so on are increasing in importance. The application of big data and AI to manufacturing, smart logistics and health care is quite widespread.

China is leading in smart manufacturing, implementing complex designs in mass production via precision engineering at high speeds and at low costs. By 2020, China had built 11 'lighthouse factories' — benchmark smart manufacturers — claiming the top ranking on the World Economic Forum's 'global lighthouse network'. Machine learning and big data analytics are being used to innovate in multiple fields including pharmaceutical drug design and autonomous vehicles by China's tech giants, such as Alibaba, Tencent and Huawei. In the face of rising restrictions by the Global North on trade as well as in technology sharing, China is now investing vast resources to make all the semiconductors it needs.[29]

Although China has eclipsed the United States in the number of scientific publications and patents, it still lags behind in the following respects:[30]

- China's publications reflect quantity but not necessarily high quality research, with the most cited publications being from the United States.
- The fraction of R&D in fundamental as opposed to applied research still lags behind the Global North.
- The science, technology, engineering, and mathematics (STEM) graduates outnumber the Global North, but still lack top-tier talent in high-tech and emerging disciplines, such as AI and semiconductors.
- The quality of patents measured by their scientific impact and commercialization potential is still behind China's international competitors.

3.10 China's Meteoric Rise

Macroeconomic data provides empirical evidence of the comprehensive and sustained development of China's economy. All the macroeconomic indicators discussed in Section 3.2, in particular the GDP figures shown in Figure 3.1, point to the rapid expansion of China's economy.

In 1949, China started from an economically backward agricultural and feudal society. The 1979 economic reforms and 'opening up' has led to its rapid growth, starting in 1990. Besides the decisions taken after 1979, as mentioned earlier, two other factors were the basis of China's rapid rise: (a) the legacy of human capital from pre-modern China, discussed in Section 6.5 of Chapter 6 and (b) the foundations of the economy laid in the first 30 years of the PRC, from 1949 to 1979, discussed in Section 10.2 of Chapter 10.

By 2019, China had become an economic heavyweight, a leading tech innovator and the fastest growing and most important growth engine of the world [1]. The rise of China has also brought balance to the world's political and economic landscape that for the last three centuries had been dominated by the Global North.

The principles and policies of China's economic model and its macroeconomy are summarized. It is worth noting that China has created a unique path for its socio-economic ascension by pioneering its own innovative development paradigms. Some social and economic indicators of China's rise are the following [14]:

- From 1978 to 2019, according to the World Bank, the number of people in China living below the international poverty line dropped by more than 850 million [14], with another 99 million people being brought out of poverty by 2021.[31]
- China has uplifted, socially and economically, 800 million people — an unequaled historic achievement. The middle class has grown from 80 million in 2002 to 400 million in 2019.[32] Some sources put the estimate of China's middle class to be 700 million in 2020.[33]
- The life expectancy in China has increased by 35 years, from 42 years in 1949 to 77 years in 2018.
- The average annual Chinese disposable per capita income has been on the rise from 98 yuan in 1956 to 171 yuan in 1978 to 28,228 yuan in 2018 [14].
- In 2020, China was globally the biggest trading nation, with exports and imports given by $2.6 trillion and $2.1 trillion, respectively. In comparison, the United States exports and imports in

2020 were $1.6 trillion and $2.4 trillion, respectively.[34] China is projected to increase its total foreign trade to $5.1 trillion by 2025.[35]

- In 2020, China was the biggest trading partner of over 120 countries with its trade surplus reaching $535 billion, a 27% increase from 2019.[36]
- China overtook the United States, in 2019, to become the world's largest retail market of consumer goods, which was worth $6.3 trillion in 2019.[37]
- In 2020, China was the biggest recipient of $163 billion inflow of foreign direct investment (FDI), higher that the $134 billion attracted by the United States, reflecting the confidence of the global investors in the future of China.[38] In 2021, the FDI inflows came in at $173.48 billion, up 20.2% year on year.[39]
- China's foreign exchange reserves of $3.22 trillion in October 2021 was the highest in the world, and its gold reserves were $110.45 billion.[40]
- A 2022 research report by McKinsey and Company shows that the world's wealth rose to $514 trillion at the end of 2020. The report states that China's wealth reached $120 trillion in 2020, surpassing the United States' wealth of $90 trillion. The report noted that in two decades, China's wealth made a jump of $113 trillion to $120 trillion from just $7 trillion in 2000.[41]

Endnotes

[1] https://www.un.org/press/en/2019/sgsm19779.doc.htm.

[2] https://read.oecd-library.org/development/chinese-economic-performance-in-the-long-run-\960-2030-ad-second-edition-revised-and-updated/economic-decli ne-and-external-humiliation-\1820-1949_9789264037632-3-en#page2.

[3] https://news.cgtn.com/news/2019-09-27/China-issues-white-paper-on-China-and-world-in-new-era-Kk2Nk6ja2k/index.html.

[4] https://www.scmp.com/economy/china-economy/article/3085501/china-over takes-us-no-1-buying-power-still-clings-developing.

[5] M2 is a calculation of the money supply that includes all cash, checking deposits, savings deposits, money market securities, and other time deposits.

[6] https://www.globaltimes.cn/page/202111/1237852.shtml.

[7] https://www.nytimes.com/2013/01/17/business/chinas-ambitious-goal-for-boom-in-college-graduates.html.

[8]https://www.studyinchina.com.my/web/page/chinas-investment-in-universities-pays-off/.

[9]https://www.statista.com/statistics/227272/number-of-university-graduates-in-china/.

[10]https://news.cgtn.com/news/2019-09-27/China-issues-white-paper-on-China-and-world-in-new-era-Kk2Nk6ja2k/index.html.

[11]https://enapp.globaltimes.cn/article/1243015.

[12]https://www.globaltimes.cn/content/1165370.shtml.

[13]https://www.imf.org/EXTERNAL/PUBS/FT/ISSUES8/INDEX.HTM;
https://data.worldbank.org/indicator/SL.AGR.EMPL.ZS?locations=CN.

[14]https://www.theglobaleconomy.com/South-Korea/rural_population_percent/
#:~:text\=The%20latest%20value%20from%202021,to%20compare%20trends%
20over%20time.

[15]https://data.worldbank.org/indicator/SL.AGR.EMPL.ZS?locations=CN.

[16]https://asiatimes.com/2021/10/china-marches-on-towards-fourth-industrial-revolution/?mc_cid=988992ea06&mc_eid=dcc534b51c.

[17]https://www.globaltimes.cn/page/200908/458992.shtml.

[18]https://www.theguardian.com/us-news/2019/aug/23/trump-china-economic-war-why-reasons.

[19]https://data.worldbank.org/indicator/NY.GDS.TOTL.ZS?end=2020&
locations=CN&start=1960.

[20]file:///C:/Users/BEBaaquie/Downloads/Reform%20Success%20of%20China
%20FINAL.pdf.

[21]https://global.chinadaily.com.cn/a/202011/09/WS5fa89793a31024ad0ba83e03_
1.html.

[22]https://enapp.globaltimes.cn/article/1267795.

[23]https://www.globaltimes.cn/page/202206/1268126.shtml.

[24]http://enapp.globaltimes.cn/article/1230033.

[25]http://enapp.globaltimes.cn/article/1230033.

[26]https://www.globaltimes.cn/page/202206/1267437.shtml.

[27]https://www.globaltimes.cn/page/202204/1260617.shtml.

[28]https://www.statista.com/statistics/257152/ranking-of-the-20-countries-with-the-most-patent-grants/.

[29]https://theconversation.com/chinas-innovation-machine-how-it-works-how-its-changing-and-why-it-matters-180615.

[30]https://theconversation.com/chinas-innovation-machine-how-it-works-how-its-changing-and-why-it-matters-180615.

[31]http://www.xinhuanet.com/english/2021-02/25/c_139767595.htm.

[32]https://news.cgtn.com/news/2019-09-27/China-issues-white-paper-on-China-and-world-in-new-era-Kk2Nk6ja2k/index.html.

[33]https://www.statista.com/statistics/875874/middle-class-population-in-china/.

[34]https://trendeconomy.com/data/h2/China/TOTAL.

[35]https://www.globaltimes.cn/page/202107/1228262.shtml.

[36]https://www.bloomberg.com/news/articles/2021-01-14/china-s-trade-surplus-hits-record-as-pandemic-fuels-exports?&utm_source=google&utm_medium=cpc

&utm_campaign=dsa&utm_term=&\gclid=Cj0KCQjwu7OIBhCsARIsALxCUa
PtIb_pQ87h9cATVHP5CbYd916pdAa6JKQHiX2LE2srFhj-H0SoyL0aAvXkEA
Lw_wcB&gclsrc=aw.ds.
[37] https://www.chinabankingnews.com/2020/12/22/china-emerges-as-worlds-
biggest-consumer-of-physical-goods/;https://finance.yahoo.com/news/china-
overtake-u-world-largest-135614391.html.
[38] https://www.reuters.com/article/us-china-economy-fdi-idUSKBN29T0TC.
[39] https://www.china-briefing.com/news/chinas-fdi-record-high-2021-global-
fdi-rebound-services-high-tech-industry/.
[40] https://enapp.globaltimes.cn/article/1238314.
[41] https://www.globaltimes.cn/page/202111/1239481.shtml.

Chapter 4

China's Peaceful Rise

The path of industrialization taken by China, and how it differs fundamentally from the path taken by the leading developed countries, is briefly discussed. Macroeconomic data of economic and social indicators given in Sections 3.2 and 3.10 of Chapter 3 show that China has joined the ranks of the leading economies of the world. The economic rise of China was accomplished primarily in the period of 1979–2019. It is noteworthy that during this period, China had no military conflict or confrontation with any other country, and the rise was accomplished through entirely peaceful economic means.

There are two main reasons for China's peaceful rise: (a) primitive accumulation — defined in Section 4.1 — was carried out domestically and (b) globalization gave China access to markets overseas that the colonizing nations acquired by military means.

A major indicator of China's peaceful rise is that it is a global power that has peacefully established trade and commercial links with all countries of the world — going on to becoming the largest exporting and second largest importing nation of the world. This is quite unlike the model of colonization in which trade was established with the colonies by force.

This analysis does not discuss the rivalry, competition and confrontation of the United States with China as these issues are relatively recent and fall within the domain of geopolitics. The US–China rivalry started openly much after China's rise had been accomplished, with the United States' 'pivot to East Asia' started only in 2012 and with 2018 being the onset of the US–China trade war.

4.1   Primitive Accumulation

Primitive accumulation refers to the accumulation of the initial capital required for a country's industrialization: it is the necessary capital input required for transforming an agriculture-based subsistence economy to a modern industrial market-driven economy. The accumulated capital together with the transformation of farmers into an industrial working force form the ingredients required for a country's industrialization.

Many historians, including more recently Perelman [23], are of the view that one of the main reasons for colonization is that it provided a rapid means for the primitive accumulation of capital. In the industrialization of countries such as Great Britain, France and the United States — starting from 1600 onward — a central role in primitive accumulation was played by colonization, slave trade and the exploitation of the Americas [23]. Primitive accumulation also partly explains the newly industrializing Japan's drive to colonize, beginning with the colonization of the Chinese island of Taiwan in 1895, Korea in 1910 and parts of mainland China, starting with Manchuria in 1931.

The economist Yi Wen has analyzed the differences between the industrialization of China compared with other countries. He has given a detailed analysis of specific policies, especially of the modernization of agriculture, that are at the foundation of China's rise; he has also made a comparison with the rise of other developed countries [11].[1]

Primitive accumulation in China, from 1949 to 1979, followed the model of the Soviet Union of expropriating agricultural land and products, such as grain and industrial raw materials, for the sake of investing in a centrally planned expansion of industrial production and in a growing urban population. Far-reaching and extensive reforms in agriculture freed farmers from subsistence farming and led, by 2019, to the massive urbanization of over 600 million rural population, as discussed in Section 3.6 of Chapter 3, and which completed the requirement for China's industrialization by creating a domestic industrial working class.

The Soviet Union, starting in 1929, expropriated landlords (*kulaks*) and repressed the peasantry; in contrast, from 1927 onward, in areas under its control, the CPC carried out land reforms by empowering the peasantry. The landlords were expropriated and the land was given to the poor peasants. Major land reforms were carried out from 1946 that peaked, after the founding of the PRC, around 1953, with all land being either distributed to the peasantry, owned collectively or by the state [24].

The salient point to note is that China accomplished the *primitive accumulation* of capital required for industrialization without colonization, primarily by domestically expropriating agricultural land and other resources.

4.2 Globalization

Two historical events provided China with an unexpected opportunity for entering the world market: (a) the United States restoring diplomatic relations with China in 1978 as well as lifting all economic sanctions, due to the Korean War, in place since 1953 [21] and (b) the United States-led globalization of the world economy starting in the 1990s, provided an opportunity for China to join the World Trade Organization (WTO) in December 2001.

The PRC strategically utilized the opportunities that arose due to globalization and leveraged on the world market for its domestic development. China provided, for international capital, a vast range of skilled and semi-skilled workers, manufacturing facilities, financial incentives, laws that protected investors against expropriation, lifting restrictions on cross-border remittances, protection of intellectual property rights (IPR) and against the forced transfer of technology and so on.

These policies, a vast labor force, a manufacturing infrastructure and supply chains led to major inflows of FDIs and resulted in turbocharging China's industrialization.[2] The result of these policies was that China enjoyed an export-led growth from 2000 to 2020, with China becoming the largest trading nation in the world.

For example, from 2000 to 2020, the imports and exports of China increased 10-fold and China was an engine of global growth, accounting for 30% of the world's growth for the same period.[3] The second stage of China's modernization, from 1979 onward, was based on accumulated capital generated by the output of hundreds of millions of Chinese people working in private and foreign companies as well as in state-owned enterprises.

For these reasons, the rise of China has been peaceful, since the foundations of China's rise and its continued modernization do not need colonization, which has been the norm for the major developed countries.

The WTO was established by the United States in 1995 primarily to extend the reach of neoliberal capitalism worldwide. The spectacular growth of China following its inclusion into the world market via the WTO is a major unintended consequence of the WTO, since China's economic model has emerged as a powerful alternative to neoliberal capitalism, as discussed further in Ref. [1]. With the hindsight of the US–China trade war, one can surmise that the West probably made a strategic mistake by allowing the entry of China into the WTO.

Noteworthy 4.1. Can China Continue to Rise Peacefully?

The future of the China–United States relationship has been addressed by many authors [4, 13]. Some authors have claimed China *cannot* rise peacefully, including the American academic Mearsheimer.[4] This claim was made in 2005 and has been repeated by others since then, ignoring the fact that the rise of China continues to be peaceful.[5] What is noteworthy is that these authors ignore the period 1979–2019 of China's actual rise; in the absence of any non-peaceful acts by China, these authors point to a hypothetical future in which China could become an aggressive hegemonic power.

China's rise has been peaceful since the primitive accumulation of capital required for China's initial industrialization as well as China's access to the world market were both accomplished peacefully. What China does in the future is a separate question, having little or no relevance to how the peaceful rise was accomplished.

(Continued)

Noteworthy 4.1. (*Continued*)

There is another school of thought of authors like Graham Allison [12], based on the history of rise and fall of empires, called the Thucydides trap, in which a rising power is seen as a challenger to the existing hegemonic power, often leading to war. Applying the Thucydides trap to the US–China relation is based on the false premise that China's rise is similar to the other developed countries, which were vying for hegemony to accomplish their rise.

The rise of China has already been accomplished and its continuing prosperity is based on development paradigms that have no need for military domination or confrontation with any other nation, including the United States. A war of the United States, the reigning hegemonic power, with China, according to Allison is, *not inevitable*, but only if the China–United States relation is properly managed.

4.3 China's Growth and Other Countries

The scale of China's economic growth, especially for one of the most populous country of the world with a continent-sized land mass, needs to be compared to other similar countries as well as with the performance of the developed countries. The comparison is for ascertaining whether the rise of China is simply a component of the entire world economy's growth or whether it is something exceptional.

Since 1978, China's GDP growth averaged over 9.2% annually for 42 years. This is higher than the 6.6% annual growth for 15 years in Germany starting in 1951 or the 8.8% annual growth for 36 years of South Korea. Japan maintained a higher 9.3% annual growth, but only for 23 years (1964–1987).[6] It took the US from 1870 to 1995 to increase its per capita GDP by 10-fold, but China achieved this in the 28 years from 1992 to 2020.[7] Thus, no other country, be it post-war Germany, Japan or the Asian 'Tigers' — all star economic performers — come anywhere close to the growth of China's economy.

4.4   China and the Global South

4.4.1   *China and India*

China and India are similar in many ways: both are Asian countries with comparable population and with ancient civilizations, both gained independence in the same period (India in 1947; China in 1949), and both had peasant economies. China's per capita GDP in 1949 was only $23, roughly a similar level with neighboring India for about a decade, while that of the United States was about $1,800.[8] Until 1978, India and China had about the same per capita of about $200, but by 2021, China's GDP was five times larger than India's GDP. The GDP of the two countries, both nominal in terms of US dollars and purchasing power parity (PPP), are shown in Figure 4.1.

Another valuation of GDP is based on PPP, which is to compare the cost, in local currency, of a basket of goods of the country with the cost of the same basket in the United States. The PPP exchange rate for the two countries is fixed by equating the costs of the chosen basket of commodities. PPP is useful for more accurately estimating the overall welfare of consumers in developing countries since the non-traded goods across countries underestimates the purchasing power of consumers in an emerging market. For this reason, PPP is generally regarded as a better measure of overall well-being.

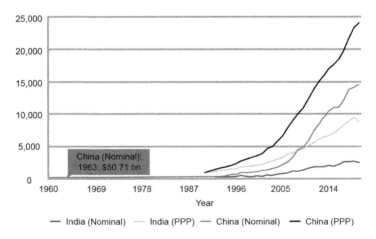

Figure 4.1.   Nominal and PPP growth of China and India.

PPP, however, is not useful for making cross-country comparisons of similar goods or for the flow of capital.

4.4.2   *China and Emerging Economies*

A few key indicators of social and economic performance are shown in Figure 4.2. All the indicators show that by around 2005 China had already pulled ahead of emerging countries that were comparable with China a decade or two ago. An analysis of three key indicators — GDP, energy consumption and urbanization — shows that by 2005 China was well on its way toward becoming an industrial nation.

An important indicator of a country's modernization is the proportion of the rural to the urban population; China has successfully transferred millions of Chinese peasantry from subsistence farming to urban industrial production, as discussed in Sections 3.2 and 3.6.1 of Chapter 3.

4.5   China and the Global North

By the end of the 2000s, China was fast catching up and overtaking the advanced economies of the Global North. Figure 4.3 shows that by 2016 the growth of consumption of China had overtaken both the European Union and United States. The second figure in Figure 4.3 shows that by 2016 China's GDP had overtaken Japan and Germany, but China was still lagging behind in per capita income and degree of urbanization.

According to the exchange rate based on import and export trade in 1952, China's gross national income was only \$18.6 billion, whereas the US' gross national product was \$351.6 billion, 19 times of China's GDP.[9] There are estimates that China's GDP will overtake that of the United States by 2026.

Figure 4.4 shows China's GDP, based on PPP, having overtaken both the United States and European Union in 2016. Based on the US dollar calculations, China has overtaken the European Union in 2021, a year ahead of previous estimates due to the exit of the UK, with China having a GDP of \$18 trillion compared to that of \$15.7 of the European Union.

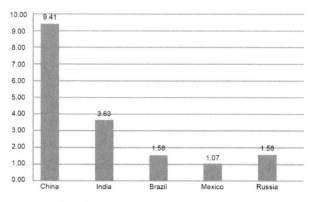

GDP at PPP in trillions of U.S. dollars (Euromonitor International, 2006)

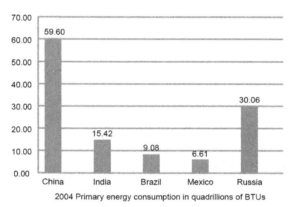

2004 Primary energy consumption in quadrillions of BTUs

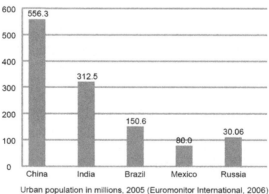

Urban population in millions, 2005 (Euromonitor International, 2006)

Figure 4.2.   Comparison of China's energy consumption and urban population with India, Brazil, Mexico and Russia.

Incremental growth in consumption, $ trillion

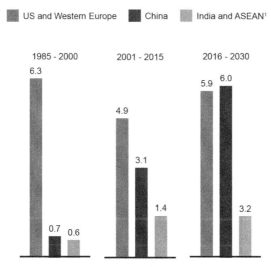

¹Association of Southeast Asian Nations.

GDP evolution by country 1960-2017,United States = 100; current $ basis

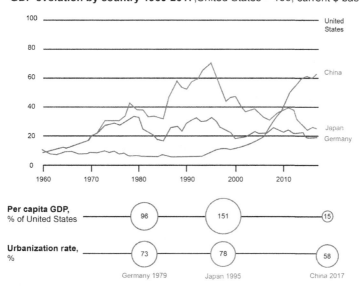

Figure 4.3.   China, India, ASEAN, the United States, Germany and Japan.

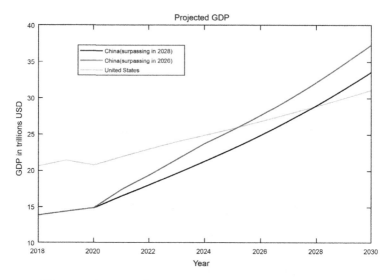

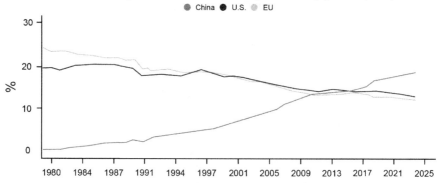

Figure 4.4.   China GDP surpassing both the European Union and the United States.

The estimates of when China will overtake the United States is a recurrent theme in the Global North, with the estimates changing on how it is calculated. The view of China on which country has the largest economy is that it is irrelevant. China's development is not aimed at competing with any country, least of all the United States, but rather has the aim of providing a good quality of life for all its people and for attaining its goal of common prosperity.[10] As discussed below, facts show that China still has a long way to go before it attains for its population the level of prosperity that is enjoyed by the people of the Global North.

The per capita income of China of \$14,000 in 2020 still lags far behind both the United States and the European Union, which are higher by about 6 and 3.6 times, respectively. However, as mentioned earlier, this figure varies depending on the exchange rates. Although China is predicted to become a high-income country in 2023, the following social indicators show that it still has to increase its per capita income substantially to reach the level of prosperity of the Global North.[11]

- China's urban housing per capita is 39 square meters, which is five times that of the eight square meters in 1978. But this is still less than two-thirds of the housing per capita in the United States, which is about 65 square meters.
- The average Chinese owns just 0.2 cars per person, a fifth of as many cars as in the United States.
- China's urbanization rate is 57%, compared with 82% in the United States. The aim of China is not to replicate the economic model of the United States, so one can expect the urbanization rate of China to be different from that of the United States.
- The average annual consumption of consumer goods per person in China is about \$4,600, which is only a quarter of that in the United States. This figure is a bit misleading, since according to PPP, the gap is much smaller.
- As of 2021, China had about 600 airports, while the United States had more than 13,500. In China, there are still one billion citizens who have never flown in an airplane.
- Only 4% of Chinese people have a university education, compared to about 25% in the United States.

4.6   China and World Economy

By 2019, the exports of China had outstripped the rest of the world in manufacturing, including the developed countries of the Global North; see Figure 4.5.[12]

A detailed comparison of China's economy with the world economy has been made in [28]. The result given in Figure 4.5 is the

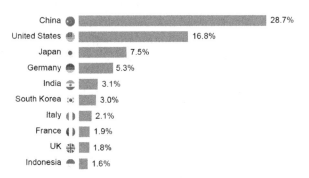

(a)

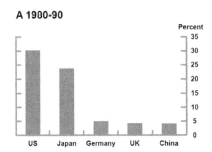

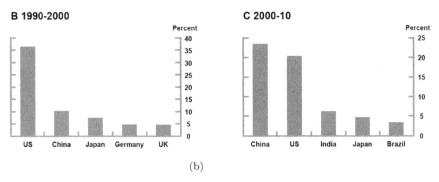

(b)

Figure 4.5.   (a) China's share of global manufacturing, largest since 2019 and (b) China and growth of the world economy.

fraction of the world's economic growth that came from different countries.

Figure 4.5 shows that, starting from a low contribution to global growth of about 5% in 1980–1990, in a matter of 30 years, China had leapfrogged and overtaken the other leading of the economies of the world, in particular the United States, Germany, Japan and the UK. By 2010, China had become the *largest engine* for the world economy, accounting for almost 25% of its growth.

A question naturally arises: What is so special about China? Why could China develop so rapidly and comprehensively compared to other nations that have been decolonized around the same time? The answer to this question is not addressed in this book and has been addressed in many scholarly publications; In particular, a detailed comparison of economic growth and sustainability in Brazil, China, India, Indonesia and South Africa has been carried out in [27].

Endnotes

[1] https://www.stlouisfed.org/publications/regional-economist/april-2016/chinas-rapid-rise-from-backward-agrarian-society-to-industrial-powerhouse-in-just-35-years.

[2] https://www.globaltimes.cn/page/202110/1236984.shtml.

[3] https://enapp.globaltimes.cn/article/1236959.

[4] https://asiapowerwatch.com/great-power-politics-why-china-cannot-rise-peacefully/; https://www.youtube.com/watch?v=YsFwKzYI5_4.

[5] https://www.e-ir.info/2019/02/21/can-china-continue-to-rise-peacefully/.

[6] https://www.globaltimes.cn/page/202107/1227540.shtml.

[7] https://asiatimes.com/2021/10/china-marches-on-towards-fourth-industrial-revolution/?mc_cid=988992ea06&mc_eid=dcc534b51c.

[8] https://www.globaltimes.cn/page/202210/1277119.shtml.

[9] https://enapp.globaltimes.cn/article/1246502.

[10] https://enapp.globaltimes.cn/article/1274841.

[11] https://enapp.globaltimes.cn/article/1259593;https://enapp.globaltimes.cn/article/1250282.

[12] https://www.statista.com/chart/20858/top-10-countries-by-share-of-global-manufacturing-output/.

Chapter 5

Summary of Part II

China has achieved great social and economic progress. Starting in 1949 from the backwaters of the world economy, China has made a **great leap forward** in its social and economic development and is today one of the leading nations of the world. There are two criteria for assessing China's progress, as discussed in Section 2.2 of Chapter 2: one subjective and the other objective.

1. The CPC has fulfilled the first centennial goal in 2021 by making China a 'moderately prosperous society in all respects' [20]. A striking evidence of this achievement is that, by 2021, China ended absolute poverty by lifting 99 million people out of it.[1] (World Bank's current definition (2022) of extreme poverty for China is subsisting on less than \$1.90 per day based on PPP, which is equal to \$1.00 based on exchange rates.)
2. The social and economic indicators discussed in Chapter 3 provide evidence on China's rise. Macroeconomic data and comparisons of China with other countries show that the objective criterion for China's rise have been met.

What is noteworthy is that China's rise has not been accomplished by colonization, exploitation, bloodshed or war, as was the case for the industrialization of the leading nations of Global North and in the rise of many feudal empires. As is clear from the analysis in Chapter 3, China's development is in step with a peaceful world and needs no war or colonization.

The transformation of subsistence farmers to industrial workers — leading to phenomenal gains in labor productivity — and the urbanization of the rural population are the key factors in China's rise. Globalization provided another major momentum for the relentless growth of China's manufacturing sector, which was also the source of massive amounts of capital accumulation due to the ongoing trade surplus. The capital accumulated by China since 1979, and in particular China's trillion dollar sovereign funds, are discussed in Ref. [1]. The accumulated capital has been employed for the overall modernization of China.

A feature of China's rise, briefly discussed in Section 3.2 of Chapter 3, Section 6.5 of Chapter 6, and Section 10.2 of Chapter 10, is the extraordinary speed of China's industrialization and modernization. This can be partly attributed to the rich legacy of China's human capital accumulated over centuries and the economic foundations laid in the first 30 years of the PRC, combined with the competent leadership of the CPC. By opening up to the world, China gained access to advanced ideas and technologies. Inviting foreign direct investments in manufacturing initiated a process of technological transfer that has continued till today, with China now reaching a point where indigenous innovation of new technologies are now coming to the forefront.

Starting in 1979, China sent out tens of thousands of students abroad for higher learning. Unlike the case of many developing countries for which the outflow of students for higher learning has resulted in a brain drain, China has had a massive brain gain, with three out of four students returning to China by 2020, as discussed in Ref. [1]. China also initiated many international scientific collaborations.

The net result of these two steps — inflow of advanced manufacturing techniques and acquiring scientific and technological knowledge — provided the foundation for developing an independent economic base for China's economic rise. As later events have shown, steps taken by the United States, from 2018 onward, to contain China's rise have not had much impact due to China's comprehensive knowledge base and domestically complete industrial supply chains.

Applying the *development paradigm of common prosperity* and transforming China into a *great modern socialist society* are the two strategic objectives and principal foundations of China's rise. In line with its development paradigms, the CPC has utilized all domestic and international factors to facilitate and enable the rise of China. The CPC is the driving force for the all-round socialist modernization of China. It has provided the framework for the opening up of China to the global economy and transforming China's macroeconomy from an agriculture-based to a modern industrial economy.

China's rise is not simply a part of the overall increasing prosperity of all countries of the world since China has outperformed both the developing and developed countries. As shown in Section 4.3 of Chapter 4, China's rise is, if anything, quite extraordinary. Having overtaken, by stages, the economic progress of all the developing countries and reaching parity with the GDP of developed countries, China is now poised to be one of the leading economies of the 21st century.

Endnote

[1]https://news.cgtn.com/news/2020-11-23/China-eliminates-absolute-poverty-one-month-before-schedule-VEp8VAJJS0/index.html

Part III
Historical Background to China's Rise

Chapter 6

Chinese Dynasties: Unification and Fragmentation

To gain a better understanding of China's rise and its governing paradigms, this chapter discusses some of the salient features of China's history. China is one of the oldest human civilizations, dating back to over 5,000 years, with earliest written records dating back to 1,600 BC and with continuous yearly records going back to 841 BC. Until 221 BC, China consisted of independent feudal kingdoms ruled by a king and the aristocracy.

The historical analysis in this chapter is largely based on the results discussed in Ref. [2]. The PRC is not a feudal dynasty, but nevertheless carries the historical legacy inherited from previous dynasties, including Confucian values, that have contributed to its rise [9].[1]

6.1   China: Unification and Fragmentation

In 221 BC, Qin Shihuang established the Qin Empire, with himself as the Emperor. He unified China by abolishing all independent kingdoms and brought the country under a single centralized system of rule. All of the Empire's administrators were appointed by the Emperor: only the succession of the Emperor was based on the blood line.

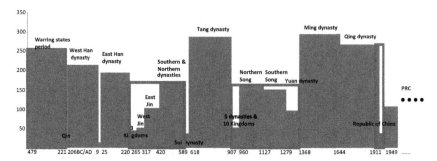

Figure 6.1.   Unification and fragmentation, and Chinese dynasties. Each rectangle encloses a period of fragmentation.

In centralizing the governance of China, Qin Shihuang abolished the system of many independent (and incessantly warring) kingdoms that had ruled China for the preceding millenniums. The system of choosing the administrators was further improved by the Sui dynasty in 621 by instituting the imperial examination system — giving rise to the scholar-bureaucrats, who were called Mandarins — which lasted for over 1,400 years until 1905.

It is discussed in Ref. [2] that feudal China had two different phases: unification (ruled by a single unified Empire) followed by fragmentation (the fall of the Empire, leading to the emergence of many independent kingdoms). Each phase of unification and fragmentation lasted for a few centuries, and the timeline of these phases is shown in Figure 6.1. If one groups dynasties that were closely related and separated by a relatively short transition period, one obtains a view of Chinese dynasties shown in Figure 6.2, with three major periods of fragmentation into many kingdoms and three major periods of unification into a single Empire. A summary of China's unified and fragmented phases is given in Table 6.1.

6.1.1   *Ancient China: Modern State or Feudalism?*

The beginning year of each unified epoch's calendar was chosen to be the unification time of the new dynasty [29]. Ancient China lasted from the founding of the Qin Empire in 221 BC until 1911, which was

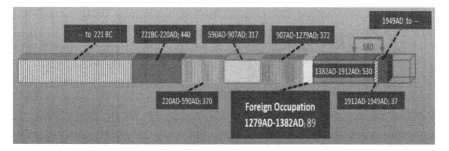

Figure 6.2. Dynasties: Unification and fragmentation.

Table 6.1. The historical phases of China. Other than a brief Mongolian occupation, China alternated between unified and fragmented phases.

#	Epochs	Phases	Start	End	Length
0	Pre-Qín	Fragmentation	—	221 BC	—
1	Qín–Hàn	Unification	221 BC	220 AD	440 years
2	Post-Hàn	Fragmentation	220 AD	590 AD	370 years
3	Suí–Táng	Unification	590 AD	907 AD	317 years
4	Post-Táng	Fragmentation	907 AD	1279 AD	372 years
5	Yuán	Foreign occupation	1279 AD	1368 AD	89 years
6	Míng–Qīng	Unification	1382 AD	1912 AD	530 years
7	ROC	Fragmentation	1912 AD	1949 AD	37 years
8	PRC	Unification	1949 AD	—	—

Note: ROC stands for the Republic of China and PRC for People's Republic of China.

the last year of the Qing Empire. There are many ways of characterizing a country's social system, and among these are two views on ancient China: that of American academic Fukuyama and the other of the CPC [31, 57]. Both of these views are analyzed.

Fukuyama's view is that since the Qin unification, China has been the first modern state; he states: *The best definition came from Max Weber: the state is about the monopoly of power over defined territories... The modern state, as opposed to the traditional state, is built upon objective measures such as equality amongst citizens...whether the law applies to those in power, whether the most powerful statesman is able to amend the law based on his interest* [57].

Fukuyama claims that the conditions for a modern state have been met by China's State since its unification in 221 BC.[2]

The view of the CPC as expressed by Mao Zedong, a founder of the CPC and the founder of the PRC, is diametrically opposite to Fukuyama's view. In his view, in ancient China, there was no rule of law and no political rights for the peasantry, who comprised over 90% of the population: *Chinese peasants lived like slaves, in poverty and suffering, through the ages...The landlord had the right to beat, abuse or even kill them at will, and they had no political rights whatsoever* [32]. Fukuyama's definition of a modern state does not tally with the facts about China's ancient dynasties since there was no rule of law nor any accountability of the Emperor or the landlord class in general.

In Mao Zedong's view, the landlord class and Emperor's autocratic rule was based on a feudal system that lived off the peasantry: *Not only did the landlords, the nobility and the royal family live on rent extorted from the peasants, but the landlord state also exacted tribute, taxes and corvee services from them to support a horde of government officials and an army which was used mainly for their repression.* [32]. Far from being a modern state, ancient China was a centralized feudal autocracy. *The feudal landlord state was the organ of power protecting this system of feudal exploitation. While the feudal state was torn apart into rival principalities in the period before the Chin (Qin) Dynasty, it became autocratic and centralized after the first Chin (Qin) emperor unified China* [32].

The term 'feudalism' characterizes a society based on the exploitation of the peasantry by the landlord class and, according to Mao Zedong, in China: *The principal contradiction in feudal society was between the peasantry and the landlord class* [32].

The CPC's armed struggle in the countryside from 1927 to 1949 was largely an anti-feudal revolution in a semi-feudal society, as discussed further in Section 7.2 of Chapter 7. The CPC's analysis of Chinese society was validated, in practice, by the successful armed revolution and the subsequent transformation and modernization of Chinese society. Furthermore, since this book's aim is to understand the rise of China from the point of view of those who wrought it, the term 'feudal' is used when referring to ancient China.

6.2 Short and Long Duration Dynasties

A closer look at the dynasties reveals that of the eight dynasties, three dynasties were short-lived, lasting for less than 40 years, and the others lasted for over 180 years. The short- and long-lived dynasties are summarized in Table 6.2 and shown in Figure 6.3.

It is important to ask: What is the underlying reason a dynasty is either short- or long-lived? Are these reasons valid for the PRC?

All the founders of new dynasties were outstanding individuals: Qin Shihuang, the founder of the Qin dynasty was a king of one of the kingdoms during the Warring States period; in contrast, Liu Bang, the founder of the Han dynasty, was born of a peasant family and was a low Qin official before he rose to the rank of a general.

Table 6.2. The reign of unified dynasties of China.

#	Dynasties	Start	End	Length	Types
1	Qín	221 BC	206 BC	15 years	Short
2	Western Hàn	202 BC	8 AD	209 years	Long
3	Eastern Hàn	36 AD	220 AD	184 years	Long
4	Western Jìn	280 AD	316 AD	36 years	Short
5	Suí	590 AD	619 AD	29 years	Short
6	Táng	624 AD	907 AD	283 years	Long
7	Míng	1382 AD	1644 AD	262 years	Long
8	Qīng	1661 AD	1912 AD	251 years	Long

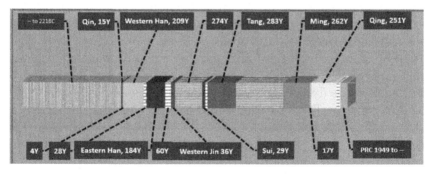

Figure 6.3. Chinese dynasties: Short and long-lasting dynasties. In PRC, the current 'Red Dynasty' rule is 73 years, as of 2022.

But the mighty Qin Empire fell in less than one generation, after a mere 15 years, whereas the Han dynasty lasted for over 200 years. The question naturally arises: what was the cause (or causes), in particular, for the fall of the Qin Empire and the success of the Han dynasties, respectively.

6.3   Pivotal Role of Second Emperor

It has been noted by historian Bo Yang that a new dynasty faces a bottleneck soon after the end of the first Emperor's rule and is long-lived only if it can overcome this bottleneck [33,34]. A detailed study carried out in Ref. [2] shows that the crucial factor and bottleneck in determining the long-term viability of a new dynasty is the *succession problem*, more specifically, the competence of the **second emperor** of the dynasty and sometimes even the third.

The reason that the second Emperor is crucial is because, given the highly centralized nature of a dynasty, the new dynasty has to face the challenge of establishing its control over the far-flung bureaucracy and army as well as take measures to bring about social and economic prosperity. Otherwise, factors like popular revolt, warlordism and other forces of fragmentation would overtake the new dynasty [2]. It is hence no surprise that, according to historians, the three most successful Emperors of China — Li Shimin (Tang), Zhu Di (Ming) and Kangxi (Qing) — were all the second Emperors.

An incompetent second Emperor can cause the new dynasty to collapse, as it happened during the Qin, Jin and Sui dynasties. Seven out of eight unified dynasties had a succession problem.[3] Four dynasties solved the succession problem and went on to last more than 200 years. Three dynasties failed the succession problem and quickly collapsed.

The Chinese dynasties covered an enormous land mass and were far-flung: for the Emperor controlling the bureaucrats, in particular for ensuring the collection of taxes, was always a challenge. The Emperor had to rely on informers and reports from low-level bureaucrats for exerting control over the bureaucracy. This was one of the systemic weakness of all dynasties.

The army posed a particularly dangerous challenge to the Emperor due to warlordism. Generals in far-flung provinces would tend to break away from a weak emperor and set up their own personal rule. The Eastern Han and Tang empires both fell partly due to warlordism [2].

Since its first unification in 221 BC, China in its unified phase was a centralized state that had two weak links: (a) the bloodline determining the succession of the Emperors could, in particular, lead to an incompetent second Emperor and (b) bureaucrats and army were supervised only by the Emperor and his immediate circle. Both these weak links could become powerful forces of fragmentation, especially once the dynasty was in decline [2].

6.3.1 *Chinese and Other Dynasties*

Each Empire in the world that rose and fell contributed to human civilizations, leaving their imprint on history. The review of China's history shows a pattern of unification and fragmentation seldom seen in any of the other Empires that lasted for many centuries. Notable among these long lasting Empires are, for example, the Egyptian Empires, Chinese Empires, Roman Empire, Byzantine Empire, Arab Empire, Ottoman Empire, Iranian Empires, Mughal Empire and the British Empire.[4] As shown by a detailed study of the last 500 years by Dalio, powerful Empires lasted about 250 years and then decayed and disappeared (except for the Ottoman Empire that lasted for over 600 years). Only two contemporary countries have seen the rise and fall of many empires over the last 2,000 years: Iran and China. Over the last 500 years, Dalio's list has three Empires in China: Ming, Qing and the current 'Red' Empire [35].

For thousands of years, many powerful empires appeared in China, such as the Qin, Han, Tang, Yuan, Ming and Qing Empires, with the latest 'dynasty' being the People's Republic of China. The rise and fall of Chinese empires, the cycle of the unification and fragmentation of China, have occurred for only the Iranian and the Chinese civilizations [2].[5] After a prolonged period of decline and fragmentation, Empires in ancient China have again risen and unified China and, according to Zhang, have rejuvenated the Chinese civilization [9].

The last instance of China's fragmentation, for over a 100 years, started with the Opium Wars in 1839 and lasted until 1949. China is now once more in its unified phase. The CPC's objective of attaining the rejuvenation of China has deep historical foundations and is one of the factors fueling the rise of China.

6.4   Chinese Dynasties and the PRC

The rise of the Communist Party of China to power and the founding of the PRC follow a pattern that has been repeated many times in the emergence of new dynasties. Furthermore, how long will the CPC remain in power — similar to the duration of a new dynasty in feudal China — may depend on factors that are in common with earlier dynasties.

Similar to previous Chinese empires, the CPC has established a centralized system of rule, and the civil servants continue to be chosen by a nationwide examination as was the case with the imperial examination system in the feudal dynasties. The dissimilarities of the PRC from previous feudal dynasties, of course, far outweigh the similarities. The PRC is not a feudal empire in which a small coterie of people centered on the Emperor rule the country, with their only claim to power being the bloodline. Furthermore, the PRC is not existing in relative isolation from the world, as did the previous dynasties for many millennia, but rather is a global player that has to contend with equally, if not more, powerful countries.

Unlike the feudal rulers of Chinese dynasties, the outlook of the CPC is not solely based on traditional Confucian values but has a broader basis, being founded and based on Marxism–Leninism. Xi Jinping stated the following: *Marxism is the fundamental guiding ideology upon which our Party and country are founded; it is the very soul of our Party and the banner under which it strives.*[6] The writings and speeches of CPC leaders, including Xi Jinping, demonstrate that the CPC has an internationalist outlook based on China's concrete conditions [19]. The social system for the People's Republic of China that the CPC is working toward is that of a modern socialist country with Chinese characteristics.

As discussed earlier, a bad second or third Emperor could lead to the fall of a newly founded empire due to the incompetence of the Emperor. As discussed in later Chapters, the CPC could stabilize its governance of China due to Deng Xiaoping being an outstanding 'second Emperor'. Palace intrigues and rivalries revolving around succession internally weakened many dynasties and also led to the downfall of a few. Factionalism in the Party is one of the major factors that, if uncontrolled, could lead to the downfall of the CPC. Once a dynasty crossed the bottleneck of proper succession, it was stable over many centuries. This is a future trajectory that seems to have become possible for the CPC.

The main takeaways from this brief summary of dynastic rule of China are the following:

1. Even though the feudal dynasties and the PRC are vastly different, some of their features are similar.
2. The centralized system of governance of Chinese empires survived — in spite of many fragmentations — for 2,300 years from the Qin unification in 221 BC up till the end of the Qing dynasty in 1911.
3. A competent second Emperor was the key link for a new feudal dynasty to stabilize and be a long-lasting dynasty.
4. A weak link of the centralized empire was the appointment of Emperors based on the bloodline.
5. Another fundamental flaw and weakness of feudal empires was inadequate and lax supervision of bureaucrats and generals by the Emperor, especially given the far-flung nature of Chinese empires.
6. Once a new dynasty stabilized, the competence of the Emperor became less important since the country would be administered by the Mandarins.

6.5   China's Legacy of Human Capital

One of the defining features of China's rise is the sheer speed at which it has progressed. The PRC has mastered myriad lines of modern manufacturing, creating comprehensive and complete supply chains for all facets of industrial production. China is now rapidly mastering advanced science and technology, as discussed in Section 3.10 of Chapter 3.

A logical question that arises is: How could China rise so rapidly? This question has been partly addressed in Section 2.2 of Chapter 2, and one needs to add a historical dimension to this analysis. The following are some social features of ancient China that bear on China's rapid rise:

1. **Inventions**: Paper-making, printing, gunpowder and the compass are four great inventions of ancient China, along with many other innovations, such as silk and ceramics.
2. **Centralized civil servants**: Mandarins (bureaucrats) were recruited largely based on merit through the imperial examination and provided an advanced system of administration not found in other feudal countries and which is well suited for modern societies.
3. **Widespread education**: The competitive nationwide imperial examination system for appointment as Mandarins led to a widespread educational system. This had the side effect of a respect for education, which was further reinforced by China's traditional Confucian values.
4. **Public works**: For centuries, many public works were undertaken, such as the Great Wall of China (220 BC, 21,196 km long). The Great Canal (1,794 km long) was started in 468 BC and was built in three stages, ending in 1368.
5. **Highly skilled workers**: Public works required a skilled group of masons, artisans, and so on with a wide range of expertise, which continued through all the phases of China's history. A large collection of skilled craftsmen were part of the feudal system for public works, constructing roads, buildings, monuments and palaces.
6. **Concentration of skilled workers**: In response to horsemen invaders from the north and west, the Han Chinese population would migrate south. Most invasions stopped north of the Yangtze river, which served as a natural barrier to the invaders, since horses could not be transported across a very wide river. This led to the concentration, in the south of China, of many trained artisans, masons and craftsmen and a continuity of their skills.

The factors above are a few of feudal China's legacy of social, intellectual and skill-based human capital that the PRC inherited. The centuries long accumulation of human capital over a wide spectrum of skills provided fertile ground for the rapid assimilation of new knowledge and for acquiring the skills required for modern industrial production.

One can surmise that the feudal legacy of human capital contributed to China's *rapid* all-round industrialization and technological ascendance.

Endnotes

[1]https://news.cgtn.com/news/78457a4d32457a6333566d54/index.html.
[2]http://www.oir.pku.edu.cn/info/1163/3097.htm.
[3]The only exception is the Eastern Hàn Dynasty, which was the shortest of the long-lived dynasties.
[4]https://www.visualcapitalist.com/wp-content/uploads/2017/11/histomap-big.html.
[5]http://www.mrglobalization.com/globalisation-winners/502-understanding-the-rise-of-china-martin-jacques;   https://opexsociety.org/thought-food/martin-jacques-understanding-rise-china/.
[6]http://enapp.globaltimes.cn/article/1227574.

Chapter 7

Rise of the Communist Party of China

7.1 Historical Precursors of the CPC

To understand the rise of the Communist Party of China (CPC), it is important to know the history of the CPC and how it has reached its present state. The complete history of the CPC is a complex and long subject, and instead of trying to cover this topic comprehensively, a brief summary is given of a few important events in the CPC's history, as these events shed light on the nature of the CPC and on its mission. The milestones of the Chinese revolution and the role of the CPC have been summarized by the CPC.[1]

The CPC led a revolution against feudalism and domestic fragmentation as well as against international forces of imperialism and domination. The CPC is the inheritor of a long tradition of peasant uprisings throughout the history of China — uprisings not matched by any other nation. China also has a long history of resistance to, and of overthrowing foreign domination. Both these factors partly explain the resilience of the Chinese revolution, although the leadership of the CPC, based on its Marxist ideology taken from 19th century Europe, has added an international ideological dimension to the Chinese revolution.

There were hundreds of peasant uprisings, big and small, against feudal landlords and the ruling dynasties, which ended in their final defeat, except for a few cases when the peasant leaders went on to found new dynasties.

A few of the many peasant uprisings are the following.

- The Red Eyebrows and the Bronze Horses were peasant uprisings in the later years of the Western Han Dynasty (206 BC–9 AD), when peasant unrest was widespread.
- Emperor Wang Mang, founder of the short-lived Xin dynasty (9–25 AD), was overthrown and executed by a peasant uprising in 23 AD.
- Famous among the peasant revolts is the Yellow Turbans uprising (184) during the last stages of the Eastern Han Empire (25–220 AD), which greatly weakened it. The rebellion was led by Zhang Jue and his two brothers and lasted for 21 years.
- Li Tzu-ch'eng and Tou Chien-teh were leaders of great peasant uprisings against the Sui Dynasty in the 7th century.
- Wang Hsien-chih and Huang Ch'ao organized an uprising in Shantung in 874 AD during the Tang Dynasty.
- Sung Chiang and Fang La were famous leaders of peasant uprisings early in the 12th century during the Song Dynasty.
- The Ming Dynasty was brought down by a peasant uprising led by Li Zicheng (1644), who was himself executed, but led to the rise of the Manchus who founded the Qing dynasty.

China has a long history of the rulers and people resisting foreign invasions. The Great Wall (220 BC) was constructed to keep out invaders, mostly horsemen of different tribes from the north. During the great periods of fragmentation of China, invaders from the north ruled China for centuries. Resistance to foreign occupation was widespread and often resulted in rebellions against it. The Mongolian occupation during the Yuan dynasty (1271–1368) was short-lived due to widespread revolts against it.

Starting in the 19th century, China was carved up into various 'spheres of influence' by the colonizing powers. The first Opium War was waged by the British colonialists from 1839 to 1842, and the second Opium War was waged jointly by the British and French colonialists from 1856 to 1860, resulting in China's defeat and China having to sign a number of unequal 'treaties'. The so-called Boxer Uprising (1899–1901) in northern China, called the Righteous Harmony Society Movement in China, was a violent anti-foreigner, anti-imperialist and patriotic peasant movement. It was an uprising primarily against foreign colonization, spheres of influence, unequal treaties, Catholic and Protestant missionary evangelism, and the opium trade. Its main targets were missionary evangelists and the colonizers.

The Boxer Uprising was doomed for failure as it was an uprising of a ragtag band of rebels with no leadership, no clear blueprint, no military training, and no modern weapons. An exception was the well-trained and well-armed Muslim Gansu 10,000-strong brigade led by General Dong Fuxiang, who were sent by a Qing general to help the Boxer Uprising and reportedly led some of the fiercest attacks against the foreign invading forces.

The Republic of China was established in Nanjing in 1912 by Sun Yat-sen, the founder of the Kuomintang, which governed parts of China from 1912 to 1949. The leadership of the Republic of China was passed on to Yuan Shi-kai, in 1913, a warlord and a Qing general who had massacred rebels of the Boxer Uprising, and China was unified under him for two years. A series of warlords occupied Beijing and several civil wars occurred during 1914–1928. After the death of Sun Yat-Sen in 1925, Chiang Kai-shek became the undisputed leader of the Kuomintang by 1926 and continued to rule China until 1949. China was divided among warlords, and it was only in 1930 that the Kuomintang gained nominal control over all of China. However, by 1927, the civil war between the Kuomintang and the CPC broke out and again divided China, which continued until China was unified in 1949.

Chinese economy had the seeds of capitalism in its commodity production, which was further impacted by foreign powers, starting from the Opium War in 1839. Foreign capital played an important role in the disintegration of the self-sufficient peasant economy as well as the handicraft industry, resulting in pauperizing large sections of the peasantry, which was the beginning of the urban working class. There was also an indigenous growth of private capital, chiefly in textiles and flour milling. All these factors transformed China's economy from a feudal to a semi-feudal economy: the society continued to see the exploitation of the peasantry by the landlords, to which other factors were added.

The imperialist powers launched many wars of aggression against China from 1839 onward. The Qing dynasty was forced to sign numerous unequal treaties, giving the imperialists jurisdiction over many parts of China and carving up the country into the spheres of influence of the various invading powers. By the end of the 19th century, different parts of China were marked off as their sphere of influence by the British, French, Japanese, the United States,

German and so on. Each of these powers occupied those areas which fell within their economic and military influence, called 'concessions', and were independent of Qing's laws. The imperialists gained control of virtually all important ports of China, which they used for dumping their goods into China as well as subordinating agriculture to their needs. They also armed many warlords to facilitate internal fighting so as to divide and rule China.

China was never fully colonized unlike, for example, India where the British colonialists occupied the country and controlled the state apparatus (1757–1947). The state apparatus in China continued to be in the hands of the Qing dynasty, but without the power to exercise its sovereignty over the colonizing powers. The actions of the invading powers dealt heavy blows to the decaying Qing dynasty and reduced China to a semi-colony, with China losing its sovereignty and independence.

7.2   The Chinese Revolution and the CPC

The CPC was founded on 23 July, 2021 (officially designated to be on 1 July) in Shanghai by members largely drawn from the urban intelligentsia; its founder members were Chen Duxiu, Li Dazhao, Mao Zedong and others. Mao Zedong went on to become the chief architect of the Chinese revolution and the founder of the People's Republic of China (PRC). The Far Eastern Bureau of the Communist Party of the Soviet Union and Far Eastern Secretariat of the Communist International (Comintern) supported the founding of the CPC. The CPC is discussed in the context of the PRC in Section 9.3 of Chapter 9. The milestones of the Chinese revolution and the role of the CPC have been summarized by the CPC.[2]

There was no precedent of a Communist Party undertaking an armed revolution in a peasant society, in particular since the 1917 Russian revolution consisted of urban-based insurrections. Marxist theory, as developed by Lenin, did not support an armed revolution based on the peasantry. The CPC's leadership had to independently develop the application of Marxism to the Chinese revolution and pioneer its own groundbreaking revolutionary path.

Mao Zedong characterized pre-1949 China to be a semi-feudal and semi-colonial country. The analysis of China being a semi-colonial and semi-feudal country led Mao Zedong to conclude that entire

Chinese nation was a force against imperialist domination, with the main vehicle of this domination being *comprador* bureaucrat capital. The peasantry, due to the anti-feudal revolution, was not a backward force as theorized by Marx and Lenin for the case of Europe, but instead was a revolutionary force. The CPC developed the strategy of waging a protracted people's war — guided by the theories of Mao Zedong that were based on the peasantry's revolutionary role — and of encircling and eventually capturing the cities from the countryside.[3]

The Boxer Uprising was a spontaneous insurrection against foreign forces; it was a precursor to the CPC's anti-imperialist and anti-feudal peasant-based guerrilla war. Unlike the Boxer Uprising, the CPC-led revolutionary civil war was carried out under a centralized leadership and guided by Mao Zedong's theories on protracted people's war, based on the premise of the peasantry being the backbone of the Chinese revolution [32].

The Chinese revolution was a protracted revolutionary war (1927–1949) of the CPC against the ruling Kuomintang and, for a period, against Japanese occupation. The feudal landlords and *comprador* bureaucrat capital were the social basis of the Kuomintang. The semi-colonial subjugation of China was aided and abetted by the Kuomintang, which colluded with the occupying imperialist powers, and accepted and acquiesced to their unequal treaties.

The civil war continued for many decades, except for a temporary CPC–Kuomintang alliance (1937–1945) to fight the Japanese army, which had invaded Manchuria in 1931 and occupied Beijing in 1937. The civil war ended in 1949 with the Kuomintang being defeated by the CPC. The Kuomintang fled to Taiwan and the CPC went on to found the People's Republic of China.

The Chinese revolution destroyed the over 2,000-year-old feudal system in rural China, which was based on the peasantry's bondage to landlords and imperial autocracy, and overthrew the rule of imperialism and bureaucrat capitalism in the cities. The CPC established the PRC in 1949 as a fully sovereign state — free from all the foreign imperialist powers that had reduced China to a semi-colony ever since the Opium War. Mao Zedong, the leader of the CPC and the founder of the PRC, can be termed as the 'first Emperor' of the socialist 'Red Dynasty'.

In 1939, Mao Zedong summed up the Chinese revolution and the state of Chinese society as follows: *The contradiction between imperialism and the Chinese nation and the contradiction between feudalism and the great masses of the people are the basic contradictions in modern Chinese society. The great revolutions in modern and contemporary China have emerged and grown on the basis of these basic contradictions* [32]. Based on this analysis, the CPC carried out an anti-imperialist and anti-feudal revolution. The Chinese revolution has been explained by Xi Jinping as a peasant-based armed revolution that overthrew *the three mountains of imperialism, feudalism, and bureaucrat capitalism* [20].

7.2.1   *Bureaucrat Capital*

Bureaucrats (civil servants) manage the affairs of a country by administering the country's state machine. The bureaucrats form a necessary component of the state machine and function according to the dictates of the ruling political power. The role and nature of the bureaucrats is determined by the character of the political power that rules the country.

China was under imperialist domination from 1839 to 1949. After the large-scale massacre of the CPC members in 1927 by the Kuomintang, as discussed in Section 9.5 of Chapter 9, the CPC came to the conclusion that Kuomintang was fundamentally a political Party that was in the service of imperialism and feudalism: Kuomintang's rule was explained by the CPC as being the dictatorship of the bureaucratic-military state machine in the service of imperialism.

Bureaucrat capital is a term used for the state-owned capital that is administered by civil and military bureaucrats with the primary objective of enriching themselves through corruption, cronyism and nepotism. The macroeconomy of the country is controlled by bureaucrat capital that exercises its control via the bureaucrats, who wield political power. There is no oversight of these bureaucrats by the people or their representatives. The judicial system is also by and large beholden to them.

China's economic system under the Kuomintang was controlled by *comprador* bureaucrat capital: bureaucrat capital that was in the service of imperialism. Comprador bureaucrat capital was the dominant form of Chinese capital, with private capital in China being a secondary and subordinate form. The cities in China were under the direct economic and political rule of imperialism and of comprador bureaucrat capital.

During the rule of the Kuomintang, a coalition of Four Families were the main local collaborators of foreign capital and, using corrupt bureaucrat capital, amassed vast amounts of wealth. The Four Families, all under the leadership of Chiang Kai-shek, were made up of members of the families of Chiang Kai-shek, Sung Tzu-wen, K'ung Hsiang-hsi and the brothers Ch'en Kuo-fu and Ch'en Li-fu. Chiang Kai-shek was married to the sister of Sung Tzu-wen.

Using the power of the Kuomintang, and in collusion with foreign capital, these Four Families established their control over the country's monopolies. In 22 years, from 1927 to 1949, they accumulated capital in excess of $20 billion. All their properties in China were seized by the PRC after 1949.[4]

7.3 Major Crises of the CPC

There were four major historical crises, bottlenecks and choke points in the rise of the CPC that could have potentially resulted in its fall; these are briefly reviewed. The CPC's views of these bottlenecks and the steps it took to overcome these crises are examined in some detail. These bottlenecks reveal the nature of CPC's leadership and its decision-making process, and in particular, its internal reforms and self-correcting mechanisms when faced with a crisis. The four crises are the following:

1. Armed Revolution, 1927
2. The Long March, 1935
3. The Cultural Revolution, 1966–1976
4. The Tianamen Square, 1989.

7.4 Armed Revolution: 1927

The decision of the CPC in 1927 to embark on an armed revolution was a watershed moment of the Chinese revolution and determined the future course of China and the CPC until the establishment of the PRC in 1949.

Soon after its founding in 1921, the CPC entered into an alliance with the Kuomintang in 1922. In particular, both the parties participated in running the Whampoa Military Academy, located near Guangzhou; Zhou Enlai represented the CPC in the academy, with

Lin Biao being among its first graduates. In 1924, Sun Yat-sen worked together with the CPC to organize a workers and peasants army for the Northern Expedition — to wage a military campaign for unifying China — against the Beijing warlord government run by Yuan Shikai as well as other regional warlords.

The Kuomintang broke the alliance with the CPC in April 1927 and unleashed 'White Terror', carrying out large-scale massacres of communists throughout China that resulted in the death or disappearance of 300,000 communists and their sympathizers [7]. It is estimated that in first three weeks about 12,000 communists disappeared or were killed or kidnapped by the Kuomintang, with CPC holding the number to be higher than 50,000. Over 4,000 communists were killed in Shanghai alone, with many of them being publicly beheaded or shot dead in the streets of Shanghai on 12 April, 1927.[5] Zhou Enlai was captured and faced execution, but managed to escape. As a result of the collapse of the Kuomintang–CPC alliance, Li Dazhao, one of the founders of the CPC, was forcibly kidnapped from the Embassy of the Soviet Union by a Beijing warlord and executed on 28 April, 1927.

The massacres of 1927 was a crucial juncture for the CPC: faced with the large-scale carnage by the Kuomintang, the CPC had to either capitulate and surrender or take up arms to defend itself and the Chinese revolution. Far from the massacres breaking the will of the CPC and making it surrender, the CPC's leadership made the momentous, historic and strategic decision of embarking on an armed revolution against the Kuomintang's armed counter-revolution: an armed revolution that would eventually lead to the destruction of Kuomintang and its rule in 1949.

In response to the massacres by the Kuomintang, Zhu De, Zhou Enlai and He Long led an armed uprising in Nanchang on 1 August, 1927, which was the origin of the Chinese Workers and Peasants Red Army, or Red Army in short, and heralded the onset of China's armed revolution. On 7 September, 1927, Mao Zedong led the Autumn Harvest Uprising in Hunan province and retreated to the Jinggang Mountains, where forces led by Zhu De converged. In 1929, Deng Xiaoping led the Baise Uprising of the Red Army in Guangxi province.

Independent revolutionary base areas were established in Hunan–Jiangxi border area under the control of the Red Army. The Kuomintang led a series of 'encirclement and suppression' campaigns by surrounding the Red base areas and creating concentric rings of concrete blockhouses (pill-boxes) of smaller and smaller radius for surrounding and annihilating the Red Army. Four of these 'encirclement and suppression' campaigns were defeated by the Red Army using the strategy of protracted peoples' war and, in particular, by the Red Army using the tactics of mobile guerrilla warfare.[6]

7.5   The Long March: 1935

In 1934, faced with the Kuomintang's fifth 'encirclement and suppression' campaign, CPC's military line — following the advice of Comintern German military adviser Otto Braun[7] — was changed by Wang Ming, the then leader of the CPC, into one of fighting defensive positional battles. The struggle of the Red Army against the fifth 'encirclement and suppression' campaign ended in failure due to the erroneous military line. As a result of the defeat, the Red Army was forced to retreat, embarking on the 12,500-km Long March in 1934 that it covered in 370 days while being pursued by a million strong Kuomintang army [7]. The route of the Long March is shown in Figure 7.1.

The Long March has been called the greatest challenge that the CPC has ever faced. Xi Jinping hailed the Long March as an *epic story written by the CPC and the Red Army, and a milestone in the historical progress of the nation's rejuvenation.*[8] Two fundamental issues were intertwined in the Long March: (a) who would lead the Chinese revolution and (b) what would be the military line (strategy and tactics) of the CPC.

In the Long March, the Red Army engaged the enemy more than 600 times, crossed almost 100 rivers, and scaled more than 40 peaks.[9] A major battle was fought along the Xiangjiang River, and more than 50,000 of the Red Army's 86,000 troops died on the battlefield.[10] Another legendary feat was the crossing of the Luding Bridge across the Dadu River, shown in Figure 7.1, which was the only escape route for the Red Army. By the end of the Long March in 1936, the Red Army and the Communist Party had lost about 90% of its members, with only 8,000 of the original force surviving, who were joined en route by others, bringing the total to 20,000 [7].

In January 1935, during the Long March and in the midst of relentless armed attacks by the Kuomintang, at a famous secret meeting held in Zunyi, the CPC's Political Bureau established the leading position of Mao Zedong over the Red Army and the Party.[11]   The

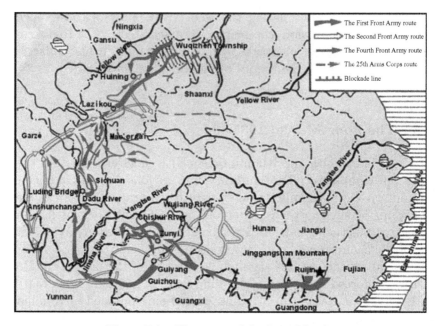

Figure 7.1.   The route of the Long March.

decision to establish Mao Zedong as the leader rescued the CPC and the Chinese revolution from defeat and made it possible for the Red Army to reach Yan'an and establish a revolutionary base area, thus bringing the Long March to a triumphant conclusion [37].

Many years later Mao Zedong made the following observation: *Who brought the Long March to victory? The Communist Party. Without the Communist Party, a long march of this kind would have been inconceivable. The Communist Party of China, its leadership, its cadres and its members fear no difficulties or hardships.*[12]

The Long March was a test of fire for the leaders of the Chinese revolution. Many of the leading members of the CPC, including Mao Zedong, Zhou Enlai, Zhu De, Liu Shaoqi, Deng Xiaoping, Chen Yun and Lin Biao, took part in the Long March. In spite of losing 90% of the Red Army and Party members, the CPC emerged stronger and more powerful after the Long March. The Long March was led by the core of the Chinese revolution's leadership, and it was this leadership — steeled and tempered by the Long March — that subsequently gave leadership to China all the way into the 21st century.

The fabled Long March was a turning point in the history of the CPC. In 2019, faced with the rising hostility of the United States and its containment of China, Xi Jinping called upon China to embark on a new Long March to break the containment by the United States, similar to breaking the encirclement by the Kuomintang. He observed that China must be clear-headed about the long-term, complex nature of unfavorable domestic and international factors and be well prepared for any difficult circumstances, adding that the most important thing for China is to do its own job well.[13]

Noteworthy 7.1. The Great Leap Forward: 1958–1961

The Great Leap Forward did not constitute a bottleneck to the CPC's governance of China since it was a mistake in the country's economic policy that was quickly rectified. The failure of the Great Leap Forward did not pose any threat to the CPC. Since it is mentioned in many discussions as one of the major mistakes of the CPC, it is briefly reviewed. A lot of literature has been written about the Great Leap Forward, including wildly varying accounts of its death toll. Instead of entering this controversy, covered in Ref. [39], one can refer to a more balanced assessment by the CPC given in Ref. [37].

The Great Leap Forward was based on the communes in the countryside and was a period of exaggerated agricultural and industrial ambitions. The primary aim was to double steel production and catch up with that of the United Kingdom. It was an attempt to industrialize using human labor as a means of replacing capital goods, which was in short supply in China. The incorrect policies were exacerbated by bad weather, crop failure and the abrupt cancellation of all contracts by the erstwhile Soviet Union in 1960.

Mao Zedong and other leaders of the CPC viewed the process of building a socialist society, after the establishing the PRC in 1949, as one where a struggle had to be carried out: but a struggle not based primarily on the laws of economics but, instead, a struggle similar to the revolutionary period, which led to an overemphasis on the subjective role of the CPC and of the people.

(Continued)

Noteworthy 7.1. (*Continued*)

This was noted in the assessment of the CPC, which had the following evaluation of the Great Leap Forward:

In 1958, ...the Party adopted the general line for socialist construction... Its shortcoming was that it overlooked objective economic laws...'Left' errors, characterized by excessive targets, the issuing of arbitrary directions, boastfulness and the stirring up of a 'communist wind', spread unchecked throughout the country...More important, it was due to the fact that Comrade Mao Zedong and many leading comrades .. overestimated the role of man's subjective will and efforts [38].

To correct the mistakes being made, the CPC Central Committee issued an instruction in January 1961 and decided on the implementation of an economic adjustment, which yielded positive results by 1965.[14]   In response to the need for economic recovery and growth, Liu Shaoqi and Deng Xiaoping scaled back collectivized farming and allowed farmers to privately farm small plots of land and sell their produce at the market.

It is an irony of history that the *Great Leap Forward* that Mao Zedong and the CPC aimed to achieve in 1960 was in fact achieved later, in the 'Great Leap Forward' that China carried out in the period 1978–2018 that left behind Europe in almost all sectors of industry, including steel production: in 2011, China was the largest producer of steel in the world, producing 683 million tons, which was 45% of the world's steel production.

The aim and concept of the Great Leap Forward was not inherently incorrect, but it was not possible in 1957, due to the prevailing domestic and international environments, to achieve great gains in output or in labor productivity. In particular, a correct understanding of the role of private capital and of the market under socialism had not yet developed. The international environment of the Cold War was also unfavorable; the economic blockade of China by the United States was lifted only in 1978 [21]. Lastly, the globalization of capital needed to be in place, which started only in the 1990s, and the opening up of China was needed to turbocharge China's economic development.

7.6   The Cultural Revolution: 1966–1976

The Cultural Revolution is one of CPC's most divisive and thorny historical questions. The setbacks of the Great Leap Forward did not create a social upheaval; however, the setbacks caused the first division among the leadership of the CPC, with Liu Shaoqi, Peng Dehuai and others criticizing Mao Zedong for the setbacks. In contrast, the Cultural Revolution, which was launched by Mao Zedong in 1966, created large-scale social disorder and chaos, and pitted him against the CPC as well as against almost all the senior leaders of the CPC.

According to the current view of the CPC, the Cultural Revolution was one of the darkest periods in China's recent history, a period when all issues in China were politicized, and the country concentrated on 'class struggle' rather than on economic development. There was large-scale chaos, and many high- and lower-ranked Party members and government officials were wronged and persecuted, including Liu Shaoqi and Deng Xiaoping.

The official view of the CPC, first made in 1978 and further elaborated in 1981, completely negates the Cultural Revolution; following is a summary of the main points [37, 38]:

- *The "cultural revolution", which lasted from May 1966 to October 1976, was responsible for the most severe setback and the heaviest losses suffered by the Party, the state and the people since the founding of the People's Republic. It was initiated and led by Comrade Mao Zedong.*
- *His principal theses were that many representatives of the bourgeoisie and counter-revolutionary revisionists had sneaked into the Party, the government, the army and cultural circles, and leadership in a fairly large majority of organizations and departments was no longer in the hands of Marxists and the people; that Party persons in power taking the capitalist road had formed a bourgeois headquarters inside the Central Committee which pursued a revisionist political and organizational line and had agents in all provinces, municipalities and autonomous regions, as well as in all central departments.*
- *... that since the forms of struggle adopted in the past had not been able to solve this problem, the power usurped by the capitalist-roaders could be recaptured only by carrying out a great cultural*

revolution, by openly and fully mobilizing the broad masses from the bottom up to expose these sinister phenomena; and that the cultural revolution was in fact a great political revolution in which one class would overthrow another, a revolution that would have to be waged time and again [38].

- *The history of the "cultural revolution" has proved that Comrade Mao Zedong's principal theses for initiating this revolution conformed neither to Marxism, Leninism nor to Chinese reality. They represent an entirely erroneous appraisal of the prevailing class relations and political situation in the Party and state...*

- *Many things denounced as revisionist or capitalist during the "cultural revolution" were actually Marxist and socialist principles, many of which had been set forth or supported by Comrade Mao Zedong himself...The "capitalist-roaders" overthrown in the "cultural revolution" were leading cadres of Party and government organizations at all levels, who formed the core force of the socialist cause. The so-called bourgeois headquarters inside the Party headed by Liu Shaoqi and Deng Xiaoping simply did not exist* [38].

The machinations of Lin Biao and the 'Gang of Four' were held responsible for the excesses of the Cultural Revolution, which was based on this group's plans to usurp and achieve complete control of the CPC:

- *In 1970–71 the counter-revolutionary Lin Biao clique plotted to capture supreme power and attempted an armed counterrevolutionary coup d'etat... Jiang Qing, Zhang Chunqiao, Yao Wenyuan and Wang Hongwen formed a Gang of Four inside the Political Bureau of the Central Committee, thus strengthening the influence of the counter-revolutionary Jiang Qing clique.*

- *As soon as Comrade Mao Zedong passed away in September 1976, the counterrevolutionary Jiang Qing clique stepped up its plot to seize the supreme Party and state leadership. Early in October of the same year, the Political Bureau of the Central Committee .. resolutely smashed the clique and brought the catastrophic "cultural revolution" to an end* [38].

The CPC's evaluation of Mao Zedong was nuanced and looked at both his negative and positive role during the Cultural Revolution. Interestingly enough, in summing up its views on the Cultural

Revolution, the CPC differentiated Mao Zedong from Mao Zedong Thought, which even till today is its guiding thought:

• *These erroneous "Left" theses, upon which Comrade Mao Zedong based himself in initiating the "cultural revolution", were obviously inconsistent with the system of Mao Zedong Thought, which is the integration of the universal principles of Marxism–Leninism with the concrete practice of the Chinese revolution. These theses must be clearly distinguished from Mao Zedong Thought...*

• *Chief responsibility for the grave "Left" error of the "cultural revolution", an error comprehensive in magnitude and protracted in duration, does indeed lie with Comrade Mao Zedong. But after all it was the error of a great proletarian revolutionary.*

• *In his later years, he still remained alert to safeguarding the security of our country, stood up to the pressure of the social-imperialists, pursued a correct foreign policy, firmly supported the just struggles of all peoples, outlined the correct strategy of the three worlds and advanced the important principle that China would never seek hegemony* [38].

The CPC concluded with the following overall assessment of Mao Zedong:

For his vital contributions to the cause of the revolution over the years, the Chinese people have always regarded Comrade Mao Zedong as their respected and beloved great leader and teacher [38].

The Cultural Revolution was brought to an end by Hua Guofeng in 1976. The CPC Central Committee resolutions in December 1978 provided the CPC's analysis of the Cultural Revolution and made economic development the primary aim of China [37]. There was an urgent need to jump-start the economy, since the working force was rapidly growing, whereas wages were volatile or frozen and the GDP was low and stagnant, as shown in Figure 7.2.

The momentous decision taken in 1978 was a critical turning point of China and broke one of the most dangerous bottlenecks that the CPC has faced. Under Deng Xiaoping's leadership, China crossed this crucial juncture by (a) rejecting the main objectives of the Cultural Revolution, (b) reforming China's economy and opening it up to the world and (c) embarking on the socialist modernization of China. The historic session became the beginning of China's reform, opening up and modernization.[15]

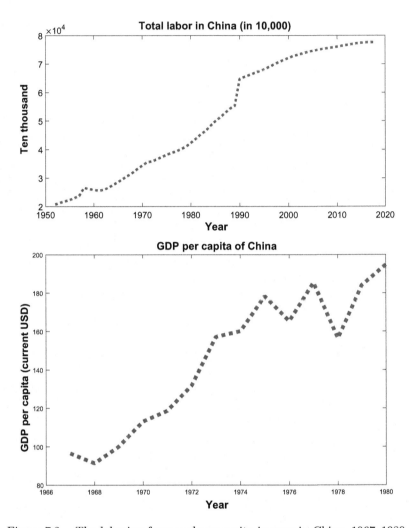

Figure 7.2.   The laboring force and per capita income in China, 1967–1980.

7.7   The Cultural Revolution Revisited

This book is written by an outside observer viewing the events transpiring in China; from this point of view, some of the extenuating circumstances and facts that seem to be relevant for understanding the Cultural Revolution are reviewed and revisited.

The CPC's evaluation of the Cultural Revolution was mainly concerned with inner-party matters and with the mistakes made by Mao Zedong. It also put on record the destructive and conspiratorial role played by Lin Biao, which seemed to reflect the emergence of warlordism in the PLA. The Gang of Four were held responsible for engaging in factional struggles, creating havoc and, after the death of Mao Zedong, attempting to *seize the supreme Party and state leadership* [38].

The reasons for the Cultural Revolution go beyond CPC's inner-party factional struggles (although these may have prolonged it), since within months of its launching, all the opponents of Mao Zedong in the Central Committee were removed. The motive for continuing with the Cultural Revolution for 10 years was clearly not a 'power struggle', as some have suggested. Following are some reasons that could have contributed to the launching of, and the prolonged duration of, the Cultural Revolution:

- **Overemphasizing the subjective factor:** Even after the setback of the Great Leap Forward, Mao Zedong was of the view — inherited from the revolutionary wars before 1949 — that one needed to make breakthroughs in socialist construction by 'continuing the revolution'. This view led to mistakes by again overemphasizing the subjective factors, similar to the Great Leap Forward, but this time not only of the CPC but of the people at large.

  The Cultural Revolution seems to have been based on a misplaced confidence in the spontaneous political consciousness of the people that in the end resulted in large-scale disorder, chaos and anarchy. With hindsight, the reforms brought about in 1979 were required for the next stage of socialist construction, as these released tremendous productive forces, which the Cultural Revolution failed to do.

- **The Sino-Soviet split:** The leader of the Union of Soviet Socialist Republics (USSR), Nikita Khrushchev, denounced Joseph Stalin in a speech in 1956. By 1960s, the intractable ideological differences of the CPC with the Soviet Party led to the formal denunciation of Soviet communism by the CPC as the work of 'revisionist traitors'. An editorial in the *People's Daily* in 1964 had the following analysis: *The revisionist Khrushchov clique knows the paramount importance of controlling state power. They need it* *for clearing the way for the restoration of capitalism in the Soviet Union.*[16]

According to the CPC, the Soviet Party had 'restored capitalism' in the Soviet Union, and this led Mao Zedong to conclude that the next target of capitalist restoration was going to be China. For this reason, a major theme during the Cultural Revolution was the need to make sure that restoration of capitalism doesn't take place in China.

It is an irony of history that the CPC was right about the restoration of capitalism in the Soviet Union; but they were 30 years ahead of their time. The Soviet Party was dissolved from within, as was the contention of the CPC about the direction of the Soviet Party, only in 1991, with capitalism completely replacing Soviet socialism.

- **Nature of private capital in socialism:** As discussed in Ref. [1], private capital was considered to be part of the United Front of the CPC during the revolutionary wars (1927–1949). Allowing private capital to function in the PRC would have been a continuation of this correct policy.

There were two mistakes made by the CPC on the economic front prior to 1966, both as a result of events in the Soviet Union:

1. The first mistake was to follow the Soviet model of having a fully planned economy with no provision for private capital.
2. The second mistake was the CPC's view that the existence of private capital in a socialist economy inevitably leads to the restoration of capitalism. It was assumed that in the Soviet Union (starting in 1956), private capital was gaining power inside the Party and would lead to the restoration of capitalism. This was possibly the reason why Mao Zedong thought that there was a 'headquarter of the bourgeoisie' inside the Party.

   Private capital and capitalism as a social system are quite distinct and discussed in detail in Ref. [1]. Furthermore, there is nothing inevitable about capitalist restoration in a socialist economy, but instead depends on the nature of the Party in power and the quality of its leadership.

The CPC didn't have sufficient historical experience for a proper understanding of the role and significance of private capital in building a socialist society. The experience of the Soviet Union after 1956 seemed to have convinced Mao Zedong that private capital would almost inevitably subvert the Party, from within, and seize state power.

The setback of the Great Leap Forward (1959–1961) and the reforms brought about by Liu Shaoqi and Deng Xiaoping to allow rudiments of a private economy seem to have further convinced Mao Zedong that these reforms would lead to the restoration of capitalism; this is probably the reason why Liu Shaoqi and Deng Xiaoping were later labeled as the chief 'capitalist roaders' during the Cultural Revolution.

With hindsight, historical experience shows that private capital is necessary for building socialism. In the fog of the 1960s, with the Soviet Union, the erstwhile leader of the socialist camp, starting to undergo auto-collapse, it is no surprise that the reading of private capital was incorrect.

However, avoiding the restoration of capitalism, which was one of the driving ideas of the Cultural Revolution, is still not a settled issue even after over 40 years of reform, as can be seen in the discussion on Tiananmen Square in Section 7.8, and on controlling corruption in Ref. [1]. The mistake made in the Cultural Revolution was that the incorrect approach of mass mobilization for political struggles without correct leadership, often leading to, anarchy, was taken to be the way of solving the problem of capitalist restoration.

With the benefit of the experience of governance of the PRC over the last seven decades, one can conclude that persisting on the socialist road cannot be achieved by mass movements and political campaigns, but instead requires strenuous and ongoing effort by an incorruptible leadership over an entire epoch. In particular, controlling corruption, especially among the top leadership of the Party, preempting the emergence of factionalism in Party, properly handling the power of private capital and so on are ongoing challenges that the CPC will continue to face for the foreseeable future [1].

- **Bureaucratism and corruption of officials:** After the founding of the PRC, the emergence of a large bureaucracy was necessary to fulfill the tasks of building a new order, and this also meant the emergence of a degree of bureaucratism and corruption. In 1966, the CPC did not have the institutions for fighting corruption, which were put in place much later in response to the grassroot demands to control corruption. In fact, the Central Commission for Discipline Inspection of the CPC was set up only in 1978, with renewed emphasis placed on its tasks as recently as in 2021.[17]

The Cultural Revolution approached the problem of corruption from a point of view that emphasized the subjective factors related to the corruption of officials instead of a systemic point of view in which appropriate institutions would objectively regulate and punish corruption. In the absence of well-functioning institutions to root out corruption, during the Cultural Revolution, a political approach was taken and the masses were called upon to root out corrupt officials and 'capitalist roaders', which in some cases lead to large-scale anarchy and chaos. In an environment of chaos and anarchy, in many cases, criminal gangs waving the red flag could gain the upper hand, causing further destruction, looting and havoc to society at large.

Rooting out corruption cannot be done by mass movements and political campaigns, but instead needs precise laws and regulations, powerful anti-corruption institutions, a long and protracted struggle, and most importantly, a consistent commitment by incorruptible leaders.

• **Revolutionary transformation of the urban population:** The campaign 'Let Hundred Schools of Thought Contend' (1956– 1957) had the intention of involving the intellectuals in the socialist society, but was brought to a closure due to the denunciation of Stalin in 1956.[18] Mao Zedong observed that many intellectuals were quite hostile to the CPC, and this seems to have further reinforced his view that the urban population, in particular the youth and the intellectuals, had not been transformed as was the case for rural China.

The CPC was the governing power in the areas under its control during the revolutionary wars (1927–1949), which were all in rural China. It was only after 1949 that the CPC gained power in the urban areas. Due to the anti-feudal social revolution, the peasantry was politically and ideologically transformed, a process that did not directly involve or affect the urban population.

One possible reason for launching the Cultural Revolution could be because China's cities and urban areas did not go through the revolutionary wars and upheavals of rural China. The Red Guards, and the youth in general, were mobilized for carrying out 'class struggle' in the urban centers. Whether these steps were well grounded or misguided is a separate issue, but one of the aims of the Cultural Revolution seems to have been to carry out a large-scale revolutionary transformation of the consciousness of urban China.

- **Revolutionary transformation of the youth and of the intellectuals:** During the Cultural Revolution, all schools and Universities were closed for an extended period, with some variation in institutions and regions. Almost all students, teachers and professors were sent to work in the countryside; trains were made free for all, from 1966 to 1969, to travel the width and breadth of China. The intention was to revolutionize the outlook and consciousness of the urban population, in particular the youth.

  Shutting down educational systems was a high price to pay and has since been criticized. But it did produce a whole generation of future leaders who had first-hand experience of the hardships and challenges of the poor and rural population, which formed the bulk of China. When these leaders came of age, it was expected that they would empathize with, and reflect the needs of, the vast majority of people.

  Whether the preparation of future leaders was one of the conscious objectives of the Cultural Revolution is difficult to ascertain. But it is a fact that many of the leaders of the CPC today are among the youth sent to the countryside, including President Xi Jingping, the supreme leader of China.

  Xi Jinping worked as the Party secretary of the village of Liangjiahe, Yanan where he lived in a cave house for seven years (1969–1976). The impact of working in a poverty-stricken village was long-lasting, since in his 2022 New Year's speech, Xi Jinping recounted this experience: *Having worked in the countryside myself, I know precisely what poverty feels like.*[19]

- **Economic base and superstructure:** Mao Zedong was an ardent student of China's history and was well aware of the cyclic nature of the rise and fall of Chinese dynasties. Among the many reasons for launching the Cultural Revolution, one more reason could have been for ensuring the long-term future and stability of the CPC-PRC by consolidating and strengthening China's socialist system.

  The economic base of a social system and its superstructure have a dialectical relation, and in general, the superstructure is determined by its economic base; this point is discussed further in Section 9.4. Under some special conditions, such as when there is a revolutionary change of a social system, the superstructure can also react back on the economic base. The Cultural Revolution intended to remove reactionary 'bourgeois ideology' from the superstructure so that it would dialectically react back and strengthen the socialist economic base.[20] The Cultural Revolution — to achieve this goal — took politics as the key link and placed emphasis on revolutionizing the educational, cultural and political superstructure of China in order to solidify China's socialist economic base and the socialist social system in general.

With hindsight, the rise of China shows that the *key link* in ensuring the long-term security and stability of PRC's socialist system is *economics*, with politics playing the leading role. Without a strong and prosperous PRC, the 'Red Dynasty' would most likely have been short-lived like many previous feudal dynasties. Although *Grasp Revolution, Promote Production* was one of the guiding principles of the Cultural Revolution, by taking politics as the key link, combined with insufficient experience for correctly understanding the role of the market and private capital in socialist construction, economic development was *de facto* relegated to having a secondary importance. This misplaced emphasis was subsequently rectified in 1979 by the CPC, under the leadership of Deng Xiaoping, with economic development being taken to be the primary task of the CPC.

Noteworthy 7.2. Leadership Transition of the CPC: 1976–1989

From 1935 and until his death in 1976, Mao Zedong was the undisputed leader of the CPC, even when he went against the Party from 1966 to 1976. Hence, the period from 1976 to 1989 was a turbulent time of leadership transition of the CPC to the post-Mao Zedong period.

Although Hua Guofeng was appointed as the Chairman of the CPC from 1976 to 1981, it was Deng Xiaoping who was the real power of the Party from 1978 till he retired from the CPC in 1992, but still continued to be influential until his passing away in 1997. Deng Xiaoping never took the position of the Party leader, but continued to be the Chairman of the Central Military

(Continued)

Noteworthy 7.2. (*Continued*)

Commission (CMC) from 1981 to 1989, a post, except for his case, that has always been held by the Party leader. It is in the capacity of the Chairman of the CMC that, in 1989, Deng Xiaoping could order the PLA to bring the Tiananmen Square turmoil to an end.

Hu Yaobang was appointed General Secretary of the CPC in 1981; he was forced by the CPC Central Committee to resign as Party General Secretary in 1987 due to his vacillating view on whether economic reforms should be accompanied by a Western-style political system, which was termed by CPC as 'bourgeois liberalization'. He was replaced by Zhao Ziyang as the General Secretary, who held this position for only two years, since he was removed in 1989 and replaced by Jiang Zemin, who continued as General Secretary until 2002. The changes in the top leadership of the CPC reflected the conflict on what should be the future political direction of the PRC, with Hu Yaobang and Zhao Ziyang supporting political liberalization and a move away from the CPC-PRC single-party state and toward a multi-party system.

Deng Xiaoping played a crucial role in removing Hua Guofeng, Hu Yaobang and Zhao Ziyang and bringing Jiang Zemin to power, thus establishing the nature and direction of the CPC for the post-Mao Zedong era. Deng Xiaoping did not relinquish his position as Chairman of the CMC until 1989 when, with hindsight, one can surmise he had concluded that the leadership transition of the CPC had been completed after quelling the Tiananmen Square protests.

In summary, in addition to economic liberalization, Deng Xiaoping provided crucial leadership in the transition of the CPC to the post-Mao Zedong era. He played a decisive role in managing the Tiananmen Square events and played a key role in the subsequent choice of the future leaders of the CPC. Deng Xiaoping's contribution to the transition of the CPC to the post-Mao Zedong leadership was probably as important as his theories on economics and politics. The choice of the top leaders of the CPC was one of the determining factors in establishing the political framework for the economic reforms and opening up of China.

7.8   Tiananmen Square: 1989

The events in April–June 1989 in the Tiananmen Square are still being debated in China, with conflicting views from those who opposed and those who supported the event as well as the view of the CPC regarding it. A detailed in-depth analysis has been given in Ref. [40]. An exhaustive list of documents related to the Tiananmen Square is given in Ref. [41].

The protests at the Tiananmen Square started with commemorating the death of Hu Yaobang, who had earlier been removed from the top leadership position. Inflation was high and corruption was rampant. The protests were against corruption of officials and autocratic behavior of bureaucrats and Party members. Hu Yaobang was not corrupt, but Zhao Ziyang was widely perceived as being corrupt, and the protests were also about having honest leaders.

Students at Tiananmen Square initially demanded that corrupt officials be prosecuted. The protests soon turned into a political movement, probably due to the interference of foreign forces, with the students demanding regime change, calling for the overthrow of the CPC and replacing it by a multi-party system, and creating what Deng Xiaoping called a *bourgeois republic, an out and out vassal of the West* [42].

Tiananmen Square turmoil was a 'color revolution' openly supported by foreign powers, with, for example, the United States imposing sanctions on China in response to the crackdown on the protesters.[21] The European Economic Community condemned China's actions, canceled all high-level exchanges and imposed an arms embargo on China that remains in force till today.[22]

Jin Canrong, a Professor from Renmin University of China, in discussing the period of the Tiananmem Sqauare, made the following observation in 2021: *If the CPC made the mistake and compromised, China might have had civil wars as well, just like the Chechen War in Russia, or might have been attacked by the West, like what NATO did to former Yugoslavia in the 1990s, or China's state-owned properties and resources might have been privatized, and Western capitalists would have plundered the prosperity of our people like what the West did to Eastern and Central European countries after the Cold War.* He went on to observe that the PRC may have even collapsed like the Soviet Union if not for the timely intervention of the CPC.[23]

It was in the background of CPC's leadership transition, discussed in Noteworthy 7.2, with a sizable fraction of the CPC supporting opposing views, that the events at Tiananamen Square took place. The protests spiraled into a major occurrence due to support from the Zhao Ziyang faction of the CPC, a fact alluded to by Deng Xiaoping: *...small factions or cliques must never be allowed to take shape in the Party* [42]. Private capital, introduced in 1979, was too incipient to have much say in the disturbances, but if these had occurred at a later stage, it is likely the demand for ending the one Party CPC-PRC state would have found supporters in private capital.

During the course of the Tiananmen Square events, it became clear that Zhao Ziyang, who had replaced Hu Yaobang as the General Secretary, was locked in a power struggle for leadership of the CPC. He wanted to increase his power and usher in political liberalization as well as tilt China toward the Western style of governance. Zhao Ziyang brought the inner-party struggle to the public domain, thus undermining the unity of the Party and creating a possible split in the leadership as well as in rank and file of the CPC.

The CPC had the following analysis of the Tiananmen Square events. *A political disturbance occurred in late spring and early summer of 1989. The Party and the government, taking a clear-cut stand against the turmoil, depended on the Chinese people to quell the anti-revolutionary rebellion.*[24]

Zhao Ziyang was ousted as the General Secretary of the Party in June 1989 and placed under house arrest, with Jiang Zemin replacing him as the General Secretary.

Two issues at the core of the Long March and the Cultural Revolution also came to the forefront in the events of 1989: (a) who would lead the CPC and (b) what would be the economic and political line (program and policies) of the CPC. In both these cases, with hindsight, facts indicate that at the critical junctures, the CPC made the correct decisions.

Deng Xiaoping was widely criticized by certain circles in China and overseas for having quelled the Tiananmen Square turmoil and specially for deploying the PLA. However, subsequent events, and in particular, the fall of the Soviet Union in 1991 showed that political liberalization and removing the CPC from its leadership position would have led to the end of China's rise. Later events in Hong Kong (2019–2020) showed that the Tiananmen Square protests could have spiraled out of control and could have even overthrown the CPC if Zhao Ziyang had been successful.

7.9   Deng Xiaoping on Tiananmen Square

The Tiananmen Square event is a good case study of how the CPC comes to recognize a problem and the steps it takes to rectify it.

Deng Xiaoping gave an extensive analysis of the Tiananmen Square events that he termed to be a turmoil and a counter-revolutionary rebellion. Following are excerpts from the Selected Works of Deng Xiaoping, with a few of the key points in boldface [42]:

One of the causes for the recent turmoil is the **growth of corruption***, which has made some people lose confidence in the Party and the government. Therefore, we should* **first of all rectify our own mistakes** *and show understanding for some of the actions taken by the masses.*

This disturbance would have occurred sooner or later. **It was determined by both the international environment and the domestic environment.** *It was bound to occur, whether one wished it or not; the only question was the time and the scale.* **That it has occurred now is to our advantage, especially because we have a large number of veteran comrades who are still in good health.** *They have experienced many disturbances and understand the possible consequences of different ways of dealing with them. They support the resolute action taken against the rebellion.*

It was also inevitable that the turmoil should grow into a counter-revolutionary rebellion. The handful of bad people had two basic slogans: overthrow the Communist Party and demolish the socialist system. **Their goal was to establish a bourgeois republic, an out and out vassal of the West.**

Another problem is that **small factions or cliques must never be allowed to take shape in the Party.** *A clique is a terrible thing that leads to many failures and mistakes.*

The outbreak of this incident has given us much food for thought, impelling us to reflect soberly on the past and the future. **Perhaps this bad thing will enable us to progress more steadily and**

even faster *than before in carrying out the policies of reform and opening to the outside world, to **correct our errors more quickly and give better play to our advantages.***

In summary, Deng Xiaoping made the following salient points, each reflecting a different aspect of the Tiananmen Square events.

- The Tiananmen Square turmoil started as protests against corruption. One can see that corruption has been an ongoing problem, increasing in significance due to the reforms and opening up. The first step for the CPC in addressing a crisis was to acknowledge and correct its mistakes.
- It was only as late as 2012, under Xi Jinping's leadership, that a massive campaign was carried out to control and punish corrupt officials. The initial single-minded emphasis on economic development probably needed to abate for combating corruption to come to the forefront.
- Events like the Tiananmen Square would have occurred sooner or later. No further explanation is provided in the analysis, but one can surmise that the domestic factors were related to the reforms. The opening up of China to the world created an international environment that provided the grounds for foreign power's interference in China.
- The fact that CPC had numerous veteran members who had weathered many storms provided a safety value and a buffer against mistakes running out of control. This was weakened considerably during the Cultural Revolution due to the towering presence of Mao Zedong, but has not been repeated since then.
- The Tiananmen Square upheaval occurred in 1989, which was the period of the ongoing auto-collapse of the Soviet Union and East European regimes. This fact further intensified the attempts by the West to make China follow a path similar to the Soviet Union and hence the larger significance of the upheaval in posing a systemic challenge to the CPC's governance of China. The PRC could have fallen and been replaced by a "bourgeois republic", which would be a vassal state of the West.
- The concerns of the Cultural Revolution seem to have surfaced, with the threat of subjugation of China by the foreign powers being perceived by the CPC as an ongoing danger.

- Zhao Ziyang had formed a faction inside the Party. This was probably one of the main reasons that the CPC could not properly manage the protests, which developed into a major confrontation by forces opposing the CPC.
- There was a recognition that CPC will invariably make mistakes that need to be corrected, the sooner the better.

In summary, the 1989 Tiananmen Square event arose due to the protests by the students being supported by workers, who were protesting against high inflation and corruption. Deng Xiaoping made the following observation. *It was determined by both the **international environment** and the **domestic environment***. [42]. One can surmise that the domestic environment indicated that the students were being supported by corrupt officials and the rightists in the CPC headed by Zhao Zhiyang, and the international environment showed the support to the students by the United States to bring about a 'color revolution'.

When it became clear to Deng Xiaoping that the protesters wanted to bring about a 'regime change', he ordered the PLA to crush the protests.

7.10 CPC's Historical Summing Up

On the occasion of the 100 years since the founding of the CPC, Xi Jinping presented a summary of the complex and long historical path that the Party has followed since its founding. This was only the third time in its 100 years history that the CPC has done such a historical summary of its evolution, the last two times being in 1945 and 1981. In 1945, it was at the critical juncture of securing final victory in the War of Resistance against Japanese Aggression, and the second time was in 1981 in the aftermath of the Cultural Revolution.

The CPC has divided its history into the four periods given in the following and has summarized the lessons from the four periods without referring to any specific event.[25]

The bottlenecks and crises faced by the CPC, three of which were discussed in this chapter, have also been included to highlight the challenges that the CPC has faced and overcome in continuing on its socialist path. The Cultural Revolution did not pose any immediate threat to the existence of the CPC unlike the Long March and the Tiananmen Square.

1. **1921–1949**: The New Democratic Revolution
   - The Long March, 1935
2. **1949–1978**: Socialist Revolution and Construction
   - The Cultural Revolution, 1966–1976
3. **1978–2021**: Reform, Opening up, and Socialist Modernization
   - The Tiananmen Square, 1989
4. **2021–**: A New Era of Socialism with Chinese Characteristics
   - Containment and repelling by the United States

Thirteen targets have been set for the fourth period, with a summary that *the Communist Party of China and the Chinese people have shown the world that the Chinese nation has achieved the tremendous transformation from standing up and becoming prosperous to growing strong.*

The document concludes by calling upon the CPC members and the people *to make tireless efforts to realize the Second Centenary Goal and the Chinese Dream of national rejuvenation.*[26]

Endnotes

[1]http://en.qstheory.cn/2021-11/16/c_682072.htm; http://en.chinaculture.org/focus/focus/2011cpc90th/2011-06/24/content_417824.htm.

[2]http://en.qstheory.cn/2021-11/16/c_682072.htm;http://en.chinaculture.org/focus/focus\/2011cpc90th/2011-06/24/content_417824.htm.

[3]https://www.marxists.org/reference/archive/mao/selected-works/volume-2/mswv2_09.htm.

[4]https://encyclopedia2.thefreedictionary.com/Four+Families+of+China.

[5]https://alphahistory.com/chineserevolution/shanghai-massacre/#The_White_Terror.

[6]https://www.jstor.org/stable/651978.

[7]https://www.jstor.org/stable/654264.

[8]https://news.cgtn.com/news/3d49444f35597a6333566d54/index.html.

[9]http://www.xinhuanet.com/english/2021-05/19/c_139955960.htm.

[10]http://www.news.cn/english/2021-10/22/c_1310260638.htm.

[11]Zhang Guotao rejected Mao Zedong's leadership and instead of heading north towards Yan'an, retreated south towards Tibet and set up an alternative 'Party Center'. It was only at the end of 1936 that Zhang Guotao's defeated army rejoined the Red Army in Yan'an. https://prabook.com/web/zhang.guotao/1723177.

[12]http://en.qstheory.cn/2021-04/14/c_610166.htm.

[13]https://www.globaltimes.cn/content/1151300.shtml.

[14]https://www.globaltimes.cn/page/202106/1227089.shtml.

[15]https://news.cgtn.com/news/3d3d514f774d444e77457a6333566d54/share_p.html.

[16]https://www.marxists.org/reference/archive/mao/works/1964/phnycom.htm.

[17]https://news.cgtn.com/news/2021-01-24/China-s-discipline-authorities-adopt-communique-at-5th-plenary-session-XjqWdSURI4/index.html.

[18]https://english.cas.cn/newsroom/archive/china_archive/cn2002/200909/t20090923_40186.shtml.

[19]https://news.cgtn.com/news/2021-12-31/Full-text-Chinese-President-Xi-Jinping-s-2022-New-Year-address-16rCojoX172/index.html.

[20]http://afe.easia.columbia.edu/ps/cup/sixteen_points.pdf;https://web.uri.edu/iaics/files/05-Junhao-Hong.pdf.

[21]https://www.politico.com/story/2011/06/house-sanctions-post-tiananmen-china-june-29-1989-057928.

[22]https://www.dw.com/en/eus-uneasy-relationship-with-china-endures-20-years-on/a-4290281.

[23]https://www.globaltimes.cn/page/202106/1225405.shtml?id=11.

[24]https://web.archive.org/web/20120601053642/http://english.gov.cn/2005-08/06/content_20912.htm.

[25]http://english.www.gov.cn/news/topnews/202111/17/content_WS61945ecbc6d0df57f98e5141.html.

[26]http://english.www.gov.cn/news/topnews/202111/17/content_WS61945ecbc6d0df57f98e5141.html.

Chapter 8

Summary of Part III

Of all the major crises faced by the CPC some were historical bottlenecks in its rise and some were more contemporary. The myriad of crises faced by the CPC bring out the self-corrective mechanism of its organizational principles. The steps it took to overcome these bottlenecks are among the salient events in the history of the CPC and throw light on the nature of the CPC and the pivotal role played by its leadership in establishing the People's Republic of China (PRC).

The historical background of China shows a recurrent pattern of unifications and fragmentations. Since its unification by Qin Shihuang in 221 BC, according to the grouping of Chinese feudal dynasties given in Table 6.1, China has gone through four cycles of unification and fragmentation, with each cycle lasting about 500 years, with the latest unified 'dynasty' being the PRC. China has had a sequence of Empires, one after another. For this reason, many scholars have pointed out that although the PRC is termed to be a country, it is more accurate to call it a civilizational state since it is a continuation of the same Chinese civilization that runs through the entire course of China's history [9].

The CPC's observations on China's history indicate that it is aware of the dynastic cycles of unification and fragmentation. In 2021, Xi Jinping raised the following question: *How can we jump out of the historical cycle of rise and fall?* He quoted the first answer given by Mao Zedong: *As long as the people can supervise the government, the government dares not slacken in its effort.* Xi Jinping went on to provide a second answer to this question: *After a century of struggle, especially with new practices (since 2012), the Party has provided a second answer: By carrying out resolute self-reform.*[1]

Most newly founded Chinese dynasties faced a bottleneck in establishing its rule. Almost all of the long-lasting dynasties had an *outstanding second Emperor* who consolidated the new dynasty and ensured the long-term stability of the newly founded dynasty. Short-lived dynasties lasted only a few years after the death of the dynasty's founder.

The CPC is the inheritor of a long tradition of revolutionary uprisings of the peasantry against feudal oppression as well as of the struggle of the Chinese people against foreign occupation and domination. This tradition played an important role in rooting and anchoring the CPC-led revolution in the mainstream of China's identity as a nation and in the revolutionary legacy of the peasantry.

The CPC faced two major bottlenecks in its evolution: one before and another after the founding of the PRC. These two major crises were the Long March (1935) — the result of the CPC embarking on armed revolution — and the Tiananmen Square event (1989). The Cultural Revolution was relatively less important and did not pose a strategic threat to the power of the CPC.

The Long March was a major bottleneck since it was a conflict about the leadership of the CPC that had a direct bearing on the strategy and tactics of the revolutionary war. The Long March opened the road to winning the civil war against the Kuomintang and defeating Japanese occupation, leading to the founding of the PRC.

Without the leadership of Mao Zedong and his theories on protracted people's war, it is doubtful that the CPC would have been victorious in the Long March and in the peasant-based armed revolution. For this and other reasons, Mao Zedong is acknowledged to be the founding 'Emperor' of the PRC who unified a fragmented China — a fragmentation that can be taken to have started with the Opium War in 1839.

By bringing the Cultural Revolution to a closure, the CPC could change its course and establish the leadership of the Deng Xiaoping.[2] The Cultural Revolution was, in essence, about deciding on China's path for building socialism. Deng Xiaoping's ascendance to the CPC's leadership conclusively settled this issue. China could embark on its rise largely due to the foundation of land reforms and other social development laid in the first 30 years of the PRC (1949–1979), as discussed in Section 10.2 of Chapter 10.

The Tiananmen Square upheaval was about the leadership and strategy of the CPC; however, this time it was not about leading the revolutionary war — as was the case of the Long March — but, instead, about the composition of the CPC's leadership as well as about the economic system for building a socialist society. Deng Xiaoping played a pivotal role in ending the Tiananmen Square turmoil by separating economic liberalization (reforms) from political liberalization as well as establishing the post-Mao Zedong leadership of the CPC. Deng Xiaoping's theories on socialist modernization, reforms and opening up to the world led to the rapid rise of China. Deng Xiaoping can be called an outstanding 'second Emperor', since without his leadership the PRC could have been a short-lived 'dynasty' similar to other short-lived feudal dynasties.

The contributions to the Chinese revolution and socialist construction of Mao Zedong, Zhou Enlai, Zhu De and other revolutionaries were recognized and acknowledged from the Long March (1935) onward; however, the recognition of the towering contributions of Deng Xiaoping came much later. It took many years after his passing away in 1997 for the achievements of Deng Xiaoping to be understood and acknowledged. He is the primary architect of policies for ensuring the PRC's long-term stability as well as ushering in unprecedented prosperity for the Chinese people.

Mao Zedong (1893–1976) founded the 'Red Dynasty', the founding 'first Emperor' and Deng Xiaoping, the 'second Emperor', internally stabilized the 'Red Dynasty'. The consensus that Deng Xiaoping (1904–1997) is an outstanding 'second Emperor', second only to Mao Zedong, seems to have been formed around 2010, when it became clear that it was only a matter of time that China would emerge as the largest economy of the world.

The 'Red Dynasty' faces external challenges in an international arena with economic and political peer competitors that no ancient Chinese dynasty faced. If the 'Red Dynasty' can stabilize its position in the world, the internal dynamics of Chinese society and the history of Chinese dynasties over the last 2,000 years seem to indicate that the *People's Republic of China looks set to be a long-lasting dynasty that should last for more or less another century.*

Endnotes

[1]https://enapp.globaltimes.cn/article/1267071.
[2]http://ouleft.sp-mesolite.tilted.net/?p=1884.

Part IV
China's State and Economy

Chapter 9

People's Republic of China

To foreground the discussion on the founding and development of the People's Republic of China (PRC), a brief analysis of China's dynastic history was given in Chapter 6. Although the system introduced by the Communist Party of China (CPC) for the governance of China is radically different from that of the feudal dynasties, there are nevertheless some features of the PRC that can be partly found in China's historical foundations.

Furthermore, to understand the PRC, one needs to know the history of the founding of the PRC, in which the CPC was the main factor. Instead of reviewing the entire history of the PRC and the CPC — a major topic in its own right — a few salient events in the rise of the CPC were analyzed in Chapter 7, including some of the major hurdles and crises that were overcome by the CPC. For these reasons, the readers are recommended to go through Chapters 6 and 7 as a foreground to the discussions in this and later chapters.

9.1 People's Republic of China

The PRC, as can be seen from Table 9.1, is a continent-sized country with one of the largest population in the world. It occupies a compact and connected landmass, and had been in relative isolation from the rest of the world up to the Opium War in 1839.

Table 9.1.   The four largest countries by land mass: European Union is included to draw a comparison with Russia and the United States.

#	Country	Area (million km^2)	Population in 2020 (million)
	World	149	7,700
1	Russia	17.1	143
2	Canada	10	38
3	United States	9.8	325
4	China	9.6	1,400
	. . .	. . .	. . .
	European Union	4.5	448
	. . .	. . .	. . .

China has been called a 'civilization state' by some historians [9] since as a historical entity, China pre-dates the modern concept of nation-state that arose in Western Europe. It was subjugated and defeated by powers of the Global North, starting from 1839 until 1949. The Chinese refer to this period of their history as a 'century of humiliation'.

The PRC was founded in 1949 by the CPC's Chairman Mao Zedong (1893–1976), the founding 'first Emperor'. He led a protracted armed struggle (1927–1949) against daunting odds for the unification and sovereignty of China, thus leading to the founding of the PRC. The founding of the PRC was termed by Mao Zedong as an epoch-making event.

The CPC founded the PRC and established a one-party state. The CPC has been the governing power of the PRC since 1949. The founding of the PRC in 1949 as a sovereign state liberated China from imperialism, feudalism and bureaucrat capitalism, as discussed in Chapter 7, and ensured that China could freely choose its path of development. The anti-feudal revolution completely uprooted China's feudal social system and overthrew centuries-old feudal bondage of the Chinese peasantry, freeing hundreds of millions of people from serfdom.

The developments during the first 30 years of the PRC laid the foundation for the reforms of 1979 that successfully channeled hundreds of millions of Chinese people into productive activities based on the paradigm of the socialist market economy. By opening up China to the global economy and allowing private capital to function along-side state-owned companies, China freed the country's innovative abilities and entrepreneurial drive, leading to a historically unprece-dented economic boom, as discussed in Chapter 3. The paradigms driving China's economic boom are discussed in Chapter 10.

The Sino-Soviet split in 1960, besides being due to ideological differences as discussed earlier in Section 7.7 of Chapter 7, was also due to the assertion of independence and sovereignty by the PRC against the dictates of the USSR.

Noteworthy 9.1. Sovereignty and the Korean War

Soon after the PRC was established, due to the Korean War (1950–1953), it faced a major challenge to its sovereignty. The Korean War was waged by China to oppose the occupation of North Korea by the United States and to protect the then most industrialized region of Northeast China. Even when China was a weak country just coming out of a prolonged civil war, it did not waver in fighting the army of the United States, which was then the most powerful in the world.

For three long years, China's People's Volunteer Army fought the United States army with only millet and rifles, sustaining heavy losses. It nevertheless pushed back the US Army from the Yalu River bordering China to the 38th parallel, which till today is the border between North and South Korea.

The performance of China's army led Joseph Stalin to stop treating the PRC as a vassal state of the USSR. Shortly after the Korean War, in 1955, the USSR returned Lüshunkou (Port Arthur), which it had seized from Japan in 1945, to China.

9.2   PRC and Feudal Dynasties

The PRC is qualitatively different from all previous feudal dynasties, having overthrown and abolished 2,000 years of feudal bondage of the peasantry to landlordism and to the despotic rule by dynastic Emperors. The PRC is nevertheless sometimes referred to in this book as the 'Red Dynasty' with Mao Zedong referred to as the 'first Emperor' and Deng Xiaoping as the 'second Emperor'.

The terms 'Red Dynasty' and 'Emperor' do not refer to the feudal elements of a feudal dynasty, such as the bloodline, the absolute power of the Emperor, or the feudal bondage of peasants to the landlords and to the Emperor, and hence these are in quotes. Rather, the term 'Red Dynasty' is used to emphasize the following similarities that the PRC shares with previous feudal dynasties:

- A unified China, similar to long-lasting feudal dynasties, is the basis of the PRC.
- All new dynasties had outstanding first Emperors similar to the founder of the PRC.
- The CPC provides centralized governance of China similar to the governance of unified dynasties. Unlike feudal dynasties, the CPC relies on political meritocracy for its governance, as discussed in Section 9.3.
- The second Emperor was crucial for stabilizing the rule of many new feudal dynasties and making them long-lasting.
- The CPC faced a bottleneck soon after establishing the PRC similar to the bottleneck faced by most long-lasting Chinese feudal dynasties.
- The CPC's 'second Emperor' Deng Xiaoping showed the way to overcome this bottleneck, which entailed finding the economic model for the prosperity of the PRC.
- For its governance, similar to the Mandarins of feudal dynasties, the PRC chooses civil servants based on a nationwide examination system.
- The CPC faces major fault lines of corruption as well as factionalism that are similar to the corruption of the Mandarins and palace intrigues of feudal dynasties.

Looking at the history of Chinese dynasties and of the CPC, as discussed in Chapters 6 and 7, respectively, the 'second Emperor' of PRC, the CPC paramount leader Deng Xiaoping, overcame a major bottleneck by rejecting a centrally planned economy as well as political chaos due to the Cultural Revolution; this bottleneck could have led to the collapse of the PRC, as was the case for many previous short-lived feudal dynasties. He introduced, in 1979, the socialist market economy opening up to the world, thus unlocking the productive power of China.

As mentioned earlier, one can surmise that without Deng Xiaoping, an outstanding 'second Emperor', the 'Red Dynasty' could well have been a short-lived dynasty.

9.3 Communist Party of China

As mentioned in Section 7.2, the CPC was founded in 1921 by Chen Duxiu, Li Dazhao, Mao Zedong, and others. The outstanding success of the CPC in developing China was recounted by Xi Jinping on the occasion of the 100 years of the founding of the CPC [20].

In 2021, the CPC had 95 million members, who are organized into about 5 million primary-level Party organizations across the country. The primary organization of the CPC at the grassroots level is the Party cell, which is created in any organization where there are three or more members of the Party. Once in 5 years, the Party holds a National Party Congress — attended by about 2,500 members — that determines the Central Committee consisting of about 300 members. The Central Committee, in turn, elects a 30-member Political Bureau, its seven-member Standing Committee and the General Secretary of the CPC, who is the supreme leader of the Party.[1] Xi Jinping has been the General Secretary since 2012.

Xi Jinping recounted in 2021 that the CPC owes its founding to the Russian revolution: *With the salvoes of Russia's October Revolution in 1917, Marxism–Leninism was brought to China...the Communist Party of China was born. The founding of a communist Party in China was an epoch-making event* [20].

Noteworthy 9.2. The CPSU and CPC: A Comparison

A comparison is made of the CPC with the erstwhile Communist Party of the Soviet Union (CPSU). CPSU was seen for many years, until the Soviet–China split in 1960, as the leading communist Party of the world. The CPSU was an urban-based Party that had the support of the Russian workers and soldiers; CPSU came to power on the basis of the insurrection of October 1917 led by

(Continued)

Noteworthy 9.2. (*Continued*)

the sailors of Petrograd, leaving out the vast peasantry from the revolution.

The CPSU led a civil war (1917–1922) and its victory led to the founding of the Soviet Union in 1922. The Soviet state was imposed, from the urban areas of Russia, on the peasantry as well as on many nationalities and colonies of imperial Russia, especially in central Asia. This *top-down* approach was probably the reason that the rule of the CPSU was heavily dependent on the bureaucracy and on the state machine.

The CPC's route to power was fundamentally different from that of the CPSU. The CPC carried out an anti-feudal and anti-imperialist revolution by mobilizing the peasantry for conducting a protracted peoples' war (1927–1949). The CPC carried out an agrarian revolution by forcibly expropriating, landlords and feudal power holders. The war against Japanese occupation (1939–1945) for China's sovereignty and national independence was led by the Kuomintang army, with the CPC having an alliance with the Kuomintang, called a United Front, to fight the Japanese occupation.

The CPC came to power in 1949 with broad nationwide support, especially from the peasantry who compose the overwhelming majority of China. The long years of revolutionary wars had churned, stirred, uprooted and overturned the very foundations of Chinese society and revolutionized the consciousness of the people, preparing them for major and radical changes in their social organization. In contrast to the CPSU, the CPC for its authority and political power relied primarily on the peasantry and on consensus and voluntary participation of the people. Hence, although the organizational structure of the CPC is similar to the CPSU, its manner of governance of the people was not imposed on them from the top but relied on the *bottom-up* support of the people.

The CPC has been responsive to the grassroots realities partly due to its deep roots in the peasantry forged during the revolutionary wars. In facing Kuomintang's armed might, the CPC had to rely on flexible and dynamic tactics, leading to an organization built on policies that would yield concrete results and respond to constantly changing circumstances. This experience was formulated, originally in 1937 by Mao Zedong, as the following philosophical principle: *seeking truth from facts and that practice is the sole criterion for testing truth*, which was later revived by Deng Xiaoping in 1979 [36, 42].

The roots of the CPC seem to have molded an organization that could change and reform itself, which it has continued to do so until the present day. In comparison, the CPSU had a more rigid, bureaucratic and unchanging approach to its governance, which is probably one of the reasons for its final collapse in 1991.

Another striking feature of the CPC is that it has been able to attract outstanding individuals as leaders and members of the Party. The Long March was a watershed moment in China's history and the leaders who emerged from the Long March were of the highest mettle, as was evidenced by the leadership they provided during the revolutionary civil war and the war against Japanese occupation (1935–1949) — as well as in all major crises of the PRC, including the Cultural Revolution and the Tiananmen Square. The CPC has continued to develop leaders through their mechanism of selection and election, and this is reflected in the contemporary rise of China — a rise made possible because the top leaders are, by and large, patriotic and competent, with corruption kept at a tolerable level [44].

9.4   CPC: PRC's Political Superstructure

A country's social system is constituted by its economic base, composed of the forces and relations of production, and its superstructure, which consists of its political power structure, state machine, culture, ideology, institutions, media and so on. Although related to economic wealth, political power is distinct from economic power. In addition to having a dominant say in the social system of a country, political power primarily consists of having control of the country's state apparatus and the country's macroeconomy: political power, in effect, determines the overall governance of a country. Political power in the PRC resides in the hands of the CPC, and a key paradigm introduced by the CPC in the governance of the PRC, absent in previous feudal dynasties, is a *political superstructure* that entrenches and integrates the Party with the state and the economy.

The CPC decides on all strategic directions and policies of the country and leads, influences, oversees and supervises the bureaucracy and army as well as all social and economic activities.[2] The paradigms for the governance of China are anchored in the nature of the PRC, which consists of the fusion of the CPC with the organs of state power and administration of the PRC, leading to the creation of a single-party state. The CPC is the political superstructure of the PRC, and this is the basis for the governance of the single-party state.

The government of China is run by the civil service that in 2020 consisted of about 10 million members with 95% of the government's leadership positions being held by Party members. The highest government position, which is the President of China, is held by the General Secretary of the CPC; Party members at different levels hold leadership positions all the way to the village grassroots level. The Chinese administrative system has six levels of administrative hierarchy: state, province, city, county, township and administrative village. There are about six to seven ranks in the government; the lowest level functionary is the village chief, who is usually also the village Party Branch Secretary. The Party has a parallel structure that mirrors the government's 27 levels of administrative offices from the village to the center of power; almost all of the leadership positions in the civil service are held by Party members.

State leaders — premiers, ministers, vice-ministers and so on — are civil servants and are promoted to higher positions after starting at the grass roots and working their way to the top. They are evaluated at every step. Since they have worked at the local, provincial and central levels, the civil servants have a comprehensive understanding of the issues and of the impact of policies and directives and can hence integrate local needs with national priorities [44].

The competence of the civil servants is a crucial component of the effectiveness of the CPC's overall leadership. Given that the PRC is a single Party state, the quality and incorruptibility of the civil servants are a direct reflection of the quality of the CPC's leadership. To effectively govern, the CPC needs to have a close connection with the people, as well as ensure accountability, competence and incorruptibility of the civil servants. It is only with the ascendance of Xi Jinping in 2012 that corruption of the civil servants has come to the forefront, and the ongoing and far-reaching anti-corruption drive has become a life and death struggle for the CPC [52].

Noteworthy 9.3. Governance — Meritocracy

The governance of a country depends on its leaders and its political system. The criterion for evaluating both the leaders and the system of governance should be based on the results that they deliver to the people and not on the promises and claims that are made by the leaders. The process of how the leaders come to power is termed 'authoritarian' or 'democratic', with 'authoritarian' implying people have no say on who rules and 'democratic' refers to leaders being chosen by a one person one vote system.

There is a widespread narrative where the PRC is termed as 'authoritarian' since it is a one-party state, whereas the United States is termed as 'democratic' since it is, in effect, a two-party system based on one person one vote. Implicit in this statement is that 'democracy' is superior to 'authoritarianism'.

The word 'authoritarian' implies a dictatorial system controlled by a corrupt and incompetent elite that rules by repression and without the participation of the people. Many regimes in the world are, in practice, authoritarian with their leaders elected by mostly a rigged one person one vote system. Many of the countries that are authoritarian states are in fact thinly disguised civilian dictatorships that are disastrously administered and are on the verge of being failed states. These dictatorial states have an economy that is run by military–civilian bureaucrats. The economic system of dictatorial states tends to be a system of *bureaucratic capitalism*, as discussed in Section 7.2.1 of Chapter 7.

Democracy can, in principle, elect competent and honest leaders; however, there is no basis to think that democracy is the only way of doing so. The lesson that one learns from a system like the CPC-PRC one-party state, which is based on political meritocracy, is that there are many ways of choosing competent and honest leaders [44]. Democratic elections, if free and fair, can be a means for peacefully removing bad leaders as well for correcting bad policies due to the pressure from the electorate.

(Continued)

Noteworthy 9.3. (*Continued*)

In spite of the positive factors of a system based on one person one vote, it has a number of shortcomings. There are two main flaws in the 'democratic' versus 'authoritarian' narrative. The first is that democracy is *not* an end in itself but is only a means for choosing leaders who are supposed to serve the common good. These leaders need to be both competent and have integrity to genuinely serve the people and not line their own pockets. Many developing countries are ruled by repressive regimes of corrupt and incompetent leaders, who are duly elected by the one person one vote system; this is well known and well documented.[3]

The second flaw in the democracy narrative is that a one person one vote system may not, in practice, be the democracy it seems to imply. The very process of election can be dominated and undermined by the entrenched rich ruling elite. The rule by the superrich is a plutocracy, which is the case in many of the developed and developing countries [16]. For example, in 2010, the United States Supreme Court, in its ruling on Citizens United v. Federal Electoral Commission, allowed corporations and wealthy individuals to directly spend unlimited funds for supporting the election of their favorite candidates running for public office.

The total spending in the 2020 US elections for the President and Senate was a historical high of $14 billion, largely due to the 2010 Supreme Court ruling, with wealthy individuals and corporations providing over 88% of the funding.[4] The result of elections in the United States, in effect, goes to the highest bidder and cements the control of big capital and wealth over the political system of the United States.[5]

Describing the CPC-PRC state as an authoritarian state is a misnomer since the power of the CPC is not based on brute force but, instead, is deeply grounded in the revolutionary process that

(*Continued*)

Noteworthy 9.3. (*Continued*)

brought it to power. The CPC is known to enjoy overwhelming support of the people; many studies, even in the Global North, have concluded that the Chinese government enjoys the trust and support of over 90% of its citizens — the highest level in the world.[6]

The remaining question is that of competence and good governance. The rise of China is a testament to the efficient and capable leadership of the CPC. This is attributed by many authors to the fact that the CPC is an organization based on only allowing, by and large, incorruptible and meritorious members to assume higher and higher positions. An in-depth analysis of the system of political meritocracy that is followed by the CPC is given by Bell [44].

All single-party states are not equal as is the case that all countries calling themselves democracies are not the same. Many single-party states consist of the lawless dictatorship of a small coterie of corrupt elites, who loot the country's wealth and enjoy all the benefits of state power. There are also one-party states like the CPC-PRC that are based on political meritocracy, which have, by and large, patriotic and competent leaders. The hallmark of a meritocratic political system is a leadership that is based on honesty, ability and integrity, and where tangible benefits are consistently delivered to the people by efficient and competent governance.

Democracy is not a means for *competent governance* being delivered by the elected leaders. Instead, according to the narrative of the Global North, democracy is about the *procedure* of how leaders are elected with the election process being more or less similar to a popularity contest. Election promises are seldom, if ever, fulfilled; for the voting population, in many cases, it is elect and then regret.

(*Continued*)

Noteworthy 9.3. (*Continued*)

A major shortcoming of leaders being democratically elected in developing countries is that in many cases, they can be bought out and corrupted before or after coming to power. Even worse, the very process of election provides fertile grounds for foreign powers to influence the elections by providing financial and other support to their preferred candidate to win in the elections. Many of the 'color revolutions' over the last few decades have been engineered by this method.

The narrative in the Global North regarding the superiority of their social system termed as 'liberal democracy' compared with China is based on two pillars: (a) The first pillar is the assumption that Global North's political system is superior to China where all major decisions in China are supposedly made by 'a single person': this has no basis in reality; furthermore, it is stated that elections are a corrective mechanism for changing incorrect policies that are supposedly lacking in China, another statement that has no basis. The self-correcting mechanisms of the CPC are discussed in the earlier chapters, and in [1]. (b) The second pillar is that China's economic system does not have a market and 'price discovery', another statement that has no basis, since, as shown in Chapter 10, China's economic paradigm of a socialist market economy provides a key role to the market.

Based on these misconceptions, the social system of China is characterized by the Global North as 'authoritarian state capitalism' instead of what it is in fact, which is socialism with Chinese characteristics that is based on a socialist market economy.

9.5   CPC and the Army

The People's Liberation Army (PLA) traces its origins to the CPC embarking on its armed revolution in 1927, as discussed in Section 7.4 of Chapter 7. The Chinese Workers' and Peasants' Red Army was founded as the armed wing of the CPC. In the course of the armed struggle carried out by the CPC, the Red Army, based on guerrilla warfare, was transformed into the more regular PLA. The official founding date of the PLA is 1 August, 1927, based on its revolutionary roots.

During the Revolutionary Civil War (1946–1949), the PLA had an army consisting of 1.27 million regulars and 2.68 million militias. In contrast, the Kuomintang had an army consisting of 4.3 million soldiers and officers, of which 2.2 million were well trained with many mechanized divisions equipped with weapons supplied by the United States, which was the main international supporter of the Kuomintang [2].

A series of epic and gigantic battles took place, which were among the largest in modern history, determining the future of China. From 1948 to 1949, three long and decisive military campaigns were carried out by the PLA. During these campaigns, the PLA annihilated 144 regular and 29 non-regular Kuomintang divisions (one division has about 20,000–30,000 soldiers), including 1.54 million veteran Kuomintang troops, and shattered the Kuomintang army. The Kuomintang massacres of CPC members in 1927 were given a final response 22 years later with the total defeat and destruction of the Kuomintang army, which fled to Taiwan in 1949 with about one million troops [2].

The history of the PLA shows that it is an army founded and fostered by the CPC that, after the establishment of the PRC in 1949, became the national army of the country. The CPC ideologically holds that the PLA is politically subordinate to the Party, continues to be the armed wing of the Party and is under the 'absolute leadership' of the Communist Party.

The Central Military Commission (CMC), the highest body governing the PLA, is headed by the CPC General Secretary, and all of its members, including all the generals, belong to the CPC. The only case where the Chairman of the CMC was not the General Secretary of the CPC was Deng Xiaoping, from 1981 to 1989, showing the great importance of this position. The Party has branches and cells in the PLA, which ensures the absolute control of the Party over the army from the highest level to the lowest level, thus mitigating the emergence of warlordism.

9.6   CPC and the Macroeconomy

The state-owned enterprises (SOEs) form the backbone of the economy and are run by the civil servants, who are mostly CPC members, with Party committees in the SOEs occupying a key role in their governance. The CPC has extended its Party cells into the private sector. The role of the Party cells is to 'guide and supervise' the companies to abide by the country's laws and regulations as well as implement the Party's policies by taking an active part in the strategic decisions of the companies [45].[7]

Figure 9.1 shows the increase in CPC's organizations in the private sector; the CPC had a negligible presence in private companies in the early 1990s. Only by 2008 did the number of CPC organizations reach about 40% of the private companies. In 2017, the CPC requested 'comprehensive Party building' in the private sector, urging both domestic and foreign firms as well as joint-venture companies to set up Party cells. Since 2018, it has been mandatory for domestically listed private companies as well as those in the state sector to establish a Party unit.

As of the end of 2019, 1.48 million enterprises and 142,000 social organizations (private, state-owned and foreign-invested firms) had set up Party committees at the grassroots level.[8] By 2020, over 92% of China's top 500 large private enterprises had Party cells; a 100% coverage is expected soon.[9]

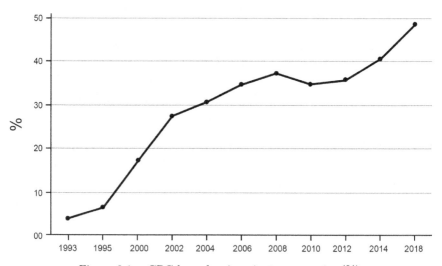

Figure 9.1.   CPC branches in private companies (%).

9.7   Historical Milestones of the PRC

The major historical milestones of the PRC, some of which have been discussed in various contexts, are the following:

- Founding of the PRC in 1949;
- Land Reform Movement, 1950–1953;
- Korean War, 1950–1953;
- Socialist transformation of ownership of the means of production, 1953–1956. Expropriation of all privately owned enterprises;
- Great Leap Forward, 1958–1962;
- Sino-Soviet cooperation and technology transfer, 1954–1962;
- Sino-Soviet Split, 1962;
- Cultural Revolution, 1966–1976;
- Establishment of diplomatic relation between the PRC and USA and lifting of all sanctions by the United States, 1972–1978;
- Economic reforms and opening up to the world, 1979;
- Tiananmen Square protests, 1989;
- China joins the World Trade Organization, 2000;
- Anti-corruption Drive, 2012 to the present.

9.8   Potential Fault Lines of the PRC

In summary, the PRC is a one Party state in which the political control of the CPC extends to all the key sectors of the social system, including the government (bureaucracy), army and economy.

The following were two crucial weaknesses of the feudal dynasties (as discussed in Chapter 6) that led to the fall of many feudal dynasties:

1. The appointment of the Emperor was based on the bloodline.
2. The personalized, non-comprehensive and *ad hoc* control over the bureaucracy and army by the Emperor created the basis of uncontrolled bureaucratic corruption as well as the emergence of warlordism.

The following is the manner in which the potential fault lines of the PRC have been solved:

- The CPC has solved a major shortcoming of feudal dynasties by freeing the succession of the Party's supreme leader from any bloodline, with the leader being chosen every 5 years by the CPC's National Party Congress.
- The political superstructure introduced by the CPC in the oversight and supervision of the bureaucracy (civil servants) and of the army ensures that there is independent control of these on an institutional and systemic basis.
- In particular, the political superstructure removes the breeding ground for the emergence of warlordism in the PLA and for uncontrolled bureaucratic corruption.

The one Party state has created new fault lines that were absent in the feudal dynasties. These are discussed further in [1].

Endnotes

[1] https://news.cgtn.com/news/2021-06-14/VHJhbnNjcmlwdDU1NjA4/index.html.

[2] The political superstructure based on the fusion of Party and the State is rooted in the CPC being a Leninist Party.

[3] https://www.transparency.org/en/about.

[4] https://www.opensecrets.org/news/2020/10/cost-of-2020-election-14billion-update/.

[5] https://www.mtsu.edu/first-amendment/article/1504/citizens-united-v-federal-election-commission.

[6] https://www.polemics-magazine.com/int/democratic-support-without-democracy-explaining-the-popularity-of-the-chinese-government.

[7] https://www.csis.org/analysis/chinese-communist-party-targets-private-sector.

[8] https://www.globaltimes.cn/page/202106/1227351.shtml. https://macropolo.org/party-committees-private-sector-china/?rp=m&fbclid=IwAR1bDHDjgNqDp9J8GwNLAbRo3hMHTktQocwJXbUb7Th08Zu0ObJ9bDuctL8.

[9] https://www.institutmontaigne.org/en/blog/influence-without-ownership-chinese-communist-party-targets-private-sector.

Chapter 10

China's Economic Paradigm

An analysis of a country's choice for its economic paradigms needs to start from the underlying premise and purpose of the country's economy. Xi Jinping has defined the following goal and purpose of China's economy: *Common prosperity is the essential demand of socialism, it is the common expectation of the people. We push the economy and society to develop, all in the goal of achieving common prosperity of the people* (quoted in Ref. [54]). For China, economic success is defined by the economy having achieved *common prosperity* for all members of society.

A brief description of socialism as practiced in China — also called *socialism with Chinese characteristics* — is required for understanding the Chinese economy. Socialism has many explanations and definitions. The primary aim of socialism is a society free from exploitation, providing for the well being of all its members by creating economic prosperity and ensuring justice and equity for all. In the words of Deng Xiaoping [42]: *The essence of socialism is establishing a just and equitable society, the liberation and development of the productive forces, the elimination of exploitation and polarization, and with the final goal being the achievement of prosperity for all.*

The feature of socialism most relevant in discussing China's socialist economy is that its strategic goal is a just and equitable economic system that aims at the optimal development of society's productive forces, in which the state is led by the working people, who are the masters of the country's wealth. In particular, for an economy based on the combination of private capital and state-owned enterprises

(SOEs), a socialist system places the people's social needs and welfare above the pursuit of profit maximization by private capital.

There are many wants and requirements of society that cannot be addressed by a social system that takes private profit maximization as its goal. For example, resources providing education and medical care for everyone, looking after the elderly and handicapped, building roads and infrastructure to distant and backward areas and so on cannot be measured by yield on investment, but instead needs to be measured by common prosperity. Society as a whole has to invest in these undertakings for the common well being of all the people.

A major litmus test of whether China is a socialist society is in the eradication of extreme poverty, since it requires that society as a whole needs to bear the burden of removing poverty. In 2021, China achieved the goal of removing absolute poverty, one of the Communist Party of China's (CPC) centennial goals. This required the strenuous efforts over many decades of three million civil servants and CPC members, as well as investments of over $246 billion. This is discussed further in Chapter 11.

The fundamental principle of a socialist society is that the wealth of the country belongs to the people. Towards this end, China has created a set of powerful SOEs that directly contribute to the wealth of the country as well as private enterprises that pay taxes on their profits. The SOEs are among the largest and most powerful enterprises in the world and are an expression of the socialist nature of China's economy, forming the backbone of the country's economy.

The discussion on China's macroeconomy, and in particular, the concept of a *socialist market economy* should be viewed in light of the *all-embracing principle and foundation of China's economy: to achieve common prosperity that encompasses all members of society.* All of China's development paradigms have been formulated and implemented with the objective of achieving common prosperity for the people at large.

10.1   Sovereignty and the Economy

An underlying template running through the entire rise of China is that it is a sovereign state that can freely choose its path of development without bowing down to any foreign power. The

Korean War (1950–1953) and the Sino-Soviet split (1960s) were both expressions of the sovereignty of the People's Republic of China (PRC), as discussed in Section 9.1 of Chapter 9. In addition to China's military power being a guarantor of its sovereignty, possessing nuclear weapons is another major pillar of China's sovereignty for the following reason.

The United States dropped two nuclear bombs on Japan on 6 and 9 August, 1945 even though it was three months *after* the unconditional surrender of Germany on 9 May, 1945. The nuclear bombs dropped by the United States showed that any challenger could face a similar fate. Hence, faced with Japan's experience and the China–United States military conflict in the Korean war, nuclear deterrence was seen to be essential for China's sovereignty. This was made even more urgent in the face of United States' ongoing hostility and a total trade embargo of China that lasted from 1950 to 1972. China acquired the atom bomb in 1964 and the hydrogen bomb in 1967.

Noteworthy 10.1. Japan, Sovereignty and Stagnating Economy

The case of Japan shows how it lacks (economic) sovereignty and hence is fundamentally different from China. Japan surrendered unconditionally on 15 August, 1945 due to its defeat in the Second World War and ever since has been under the hegemony of the United States.

During 1964–1987, the Japanese economy was growing much faster than that of the United States and its homegrown industries were dominating international exports.[1] The United States started to impose trade restrictions on Japan from the beginning of the 1980s and in 1987 forced Japan to sign the Plaza Currency Accord. This led to the rapid appreciation of the Japanese yen, making its exports more expensive. In just one year, the Japanese yen rose (appreciated) from over 250 yen to a US dollar in 1984 to just over 100 yen to a US dollar in 1985. To offset the rapid

(Continued)

Noteworthy 10.1. (*Continued*)

rise of the yen, the Bank of Japan dropped the interest rate from 5% in 1980 to a mere 2% in 1987 and later to 0%, where it has been stuck ever since, creating a massive financial and real estate bubble with devastating consequences.[2]

Japan is primarily an exporting nation, and the effect of the abrupt appreciation of the yen has been disastrous since it made all Japanese goods more expensive and hence less competitive. This led to a sharp drop of Japan's GDP growth rate from over 5% in 1985 to 0% by 1992. Ever since the 1990s and up to 2021, the Japanese economy has been stagnating at around 0% growth rate.[3]

In spite of the numerous economic measures taken against Japan by the United States — including the Plaza Accord leading to over 30 years of economic stagnation — Japan had no response to these measures since it does not seem to have the sovereign power to do so. Japan is a striking example of an advanced country that lacks sovereignty in deciding its economic policies and course of action. In contrast, for example, in the trade war being waged by the United States against China since 2018, China has waged a tit-for-tat struggle with the United States, retaliating to all tariffs imposed on Chinese exports to the United States with their own tariffs on imports from the United States. When, in 2018, the US imposed 25% tariffs on Chinese goods, China retaliated with 25% tariffs on US goods.[4]

The drastic tariffs imposed by the United States have reduced its trade deficit with China,[5] but have had a negligible effect on China's overall growth. China's exports and trade surplus to the United States have continued to rise. For example, in 2021 US exports to China grew by 21.4% year-on-year to $151.1 billion. However, the US' trade deficit with China continued to increase as well and was $355.3 billion in 2021 compared with $310.3 billion in 2020.[6]

10.2   First 30 Years of PRC

This book is focused on the historical foundations of China's rise and the emphasis is primarily placed on the era after 1979; but this does not imply that the preceding 30 years from the founding of the PRC in 1949 were 'wasted' or were in vain. The progress made in the first 30 years was the result of the founding of PRC as a sovereign country and was fundamental to all further developments of the PRC.

The PRC was founded in 1949 after a prolonged period of revolutionary wars, which was compounded by the Korean War (1950–1953) soon afterwards. China was a backward and poor peasant economy that needed to industrialize. After 1949, the PRC carried out primitive accumulation to raise the initial capital required for developing its industrial base, as discussed in Section 4.1 of Chapter 4. Furthermore, after the Korean War, the United States had sanctioned the entire Chinese economy, with the only major trading partners of China being the Soviet Union and its allies; the PRC, as a socialist country, also chose to follow the Soviet economic model. Under these circumstances, for its first 30 years, the PRC adopted a centrally planned economy.

China formulated its First Five Year Plan for 1953–1957. One of the important stages of China's economic development was from the 1950s till 1962, when China received a massive amount of assistance from the Soviet Union for its large-scale industrialization as well as *comprehensive technology transfer*. This program laid the foundation of modern technology and industry in China and promoted the development of Chinese scientific research. The Soviet technological, economic, and military aid to China benefited both nations [49]. This program had the following aspects:

- The transfer of industrial technology was facilitated by aiding in the construction of industrial projects. The USSR helped to build 156 large factories/projects, which formed the foundation of Chinese modern industry. Altogether, the Soviet Union supported 304 projects with complete equipment during the 1950s [49].
- The industries can be divided into five areas: energy, metallurgical and chemical, military industries, machine building and light industry, and pharmacy.

- These projects absorbed about half of China's total industrial investment during the period of the First Five Year Plan.
- Focus increased on developing Chinese capacity in science and technology through various forms of cooperation.
- Help was given to China to construct technology colleges, and also a large number of Chinese students were recruited to study in the USSR.
- Thousands of Soviet experts and consultants were sent to China.

The eventual split between PRC and USSR put an end to the collaboration in 1962. Although it involved some ideological differences, the main cause of the split seems to be that China wanted to fully exercise its sovereignty as well as develop its own independent industrial base.

During the first 30 years, a relatively complete industrial system utilizing the planned economy was developed. The CPC carried out extensive land reforms, built many agriculture systems like canals and reservoirs, made primary education available to all children, founded a medical care system that increased longevity, and so on. A few indicators of the progress made include the following: The life expectancy of 41 years in 1949 increased to 67 years in 1978; in the same period, the literacy rate rose from almost zero to almost 80%. Women were liberated. China raised its scientific level to the extent of acquiring nuclear weapons by 1967. China gained its permanent place in the UN Security Council in 1971.

Xi Jinping has given the following summary of the first 30 years of the PRC that laid the foundation for the reforms of 1979: *The process by which the people build socialism under the leadership of the Party can be divided into two historical phases — one that preceded the launch of reform and opening up in 1978, and a second that followed on from that event. The two phases — at once related to and distinct from each other — are both pragmatic explorations in building socialism.*[7]

The first 30 years of the PRC was the key factor accounting for the speed with which the subsequent rise of China has taken place; the legacy of human capital from ancient China, as discussed in Section 6.5 of Chapter 6, further added to the rise. Land reforms, investment in heavy industries, major infrastructure projects, such as roads and canals, the rise in literacy, the liberation of women, developing scientific manpower and so on, were essential preconditions that facilitated the rapid economic rise of China, which started in 1979.

10.3 Radical Change of Economic Paradigm

By the end of the 1950s, it was becoming clear that China's centrally planned economy was not suited for generating rapid economic growth. One of the reasons for launching the Great Leap Forward was to generate high economic growth, and its setback as discussed in Section 7.1 of Chapter 7, can be partly attributed to the fact that China had a centrally planned economy. As mentioned earlier, due to the need for economic recovery and growth, in 1961, Liu Shaoqi and Deng Xiaoping scaled back collectivized farming and allowed the farmers to privately farm small plots of land and sell their produce at the market.

The Cultural Revolution (1966–1976) was launched for many reasons, one of them being about which economic model should China adopt. The economic reforms brought about by Liu Shaoqi and Deng Xiaoping were opposed in the Cultural Revolution as 'restoring capitalism' and both these leaders were branded as 'capitalist roaders' and, as discussed in Section 7.6 of Chapter 7, removed from their positions.

During 1966–1978, there was growing social pressure on account of an increasing population and a working force that was faced with a stagnating economy — an economy that had low GDP and low productivity; this can be seen from Figures 3.3 and 3.2. Per capita income was also low and volatile, as shown in Figure 3.1 and more clearly in Figure 7.2. It was in this dire circumstance, faced with a growing danger of turmoil and social collapse, that China had to find the correct way forward.

China's centrally planned economy was taken by many CPC leaders to be synonymous with socialism. Deng Xiaoping opposed this view of socialism as being rigid and dogmatic. He reasoned that, in practice, China's centrally planned economy had not brought the expected rapid economic and social progress to China, even after almost 30 years of socialism. Although this was not stated in so many words, Deng Xiaoping was voicing the downside of central planning, which is the inability of such a system to unlock the personal initiative of the people and to provide for the consumption needs of the country's population.

To address the bottleneck in the economy, he revived the principle put forward earlier by Mao Zedong of seeking truth from facts and that practice is the sole criterion for testing truth [36]. The CPC's Central Committee meeting in December 1978 formally put an end to the Cultural Revolution (although it had been ended, in practice, by Hua Guofeng in 1976). Based on Deng Xiaoping's reasoning, the meeting made a momentous decision to alter China's economic model. Deng Xiaoping *radically changed the paradigm* for organizing China's economy by abolishing the centrally planned economy and embarking on (a) domestic economic reforms by allowing the private sector and the market to coexist with the state sector and (b) internationally opening up to the world economy.[8]

The CPC took the groundbreaking step of departing from the existing 'party-line' that socialism meant a centrally planned economy and charted out its own path of economic development. This step was similar to an earlier groundbreaking decision of the CPC, as discussed in Section 7.4 of Chapter 7, when it went against the existing Marxist views and embarked, in 1927, on a peasant-based armed revolution.

One can only speculate on what led Deng Xiaoping to propose this radical change. He was aware of the role of private capital in the Red base areas during the revolutionary wars and of allowing small-scale private farming after the Great Leap Forward. These experiences probably convinced Deng Xiaoping of the positive role that the private sector could play in building socialism in China. However, given the immense size and complexity of China, to generalize his experience to all of China required a deep understanding of Chinese society and of the workings of a socialist economy.

China could open up to the world in 1979 because, as mentioned earlier, it had reached a rapprochement with the United States. Opening up to the world economy was an acknowledgment of the fact that China needed the world market for its economic growth and modernization; furthermore, that China needed to learn from the world since it was lagging far behind the developed nations in science and technology as well as in industrial and management knowledge and know-how. By 2022, as discussed in Ref. [1], China had largely closed the gap in knowledge with the advanced countries, showing that China used the opening up for its national benefit and has not suffered from the brain and talent drain to the advanced economies that many developing countries continue to experience.

Deng Xiaoping together with Chen Yun, another Long Marcher, put forward the view that China was at a *primary stage of social-ism*, which was projected by them to last till the middle of the 21st century. The main task during this stage, as proposed earlier in 1963 by Zhou Enlai, was the Four Modernizations of agriculture, industry, defense, and science and technology.[9] Over the years, the term 'socialist modernization' has replaced the term 'Four Modernizations' and refers to the all-round and comprehensive modernization of all aspects of China. In 2022, the purpose of socialist modernization was defined by the CPC to be of achieving common prosperity, social progress, and harmony between humans beings and the environment.[10]

Figure 10.1.   Central planning of USSR versus China's socialist market economy from 1950 onward.

10.4   Rapid Economic Growth

The result of the change of paradigm for the Chinese economy led to a period of sustained economic growth. If one takes 1950 to be the beginning of post-WWII period, then, as shown in Figure 10.1, the performance of China until 1980 — due to a centrally planned economy — was as lackluster as the Soviet Union. Moreover, one can also see from Figure 10.1 that the Soviet economy dramatically fell behind in comparison with the stellar rise of China starting from 1980 onward due to the change in China's economic paradigm [55].[11]

The experience of the Soviet economy shows that, in order for China's economy to develop rapidly, breaking from central planning was crucial. The transition from a centrally planned economy to one with the market and private sector playing a key role is a complicated process. The case of the Soviet Union is discussed in Section 10.7 and shows how one could fail in making such a transition. There was a rapid take-off of the Chinese economy after the reforms of 1979, as shown in Figure 10.1 [55].

China successfully changed its economic system from a centrally planned to a socialist market economy and could subsequently provide for the consumption needs of the people. In contrast, the failure of the Soviet Union to do so, for reasons discussed in Section 10.7, finally led to its auto-collapse.

In summary, China reaped the benefits of a centrally planned economy and then, moving on, overcame a major strategic bottleneck by making a transition to a socialist market economy and opening up to the world: the transition was a historic turning point that led to the unleashing of tremendous productive forces. The first official private vendor business license was issued in 1980.[12] Reforms started in agriculture and spread to the cities. The coastal belts were opened to FDI, with the first *special economic zone* being opened in Shenzhen in 1980, allowing, for example, duty-free imports and exports.

Ever since its historic turning point, China's economy has rapidly developed, validating the change of paradigm for China's economic model. As the saying goes, with hindsight one has 20–20 vision. It is easy to see many decades later that Deng Xiaoping was correct in the historic change of paradigm that he brought to China's path of development. In 1978, it took vision to see the path forward. The social experiment that China embarked upon had no precedence and was full of unknown dangers since the results of the reforms were not possible to predict. Deng Xiaoping also had to contend with the ideological dogmatism of many CPC members that was a spillover from the Cultural Revolution.

One can only speculate that if not for Deng Xiaoping and his visionary leadership, the CPC-PRC state could have been a short-lived one, as was the case of many short-lived feudal Chinese Empires. For these reasons, as discussed in the chapter on China's history and, in particular, in Section 6.3 of Chapter 6, Deng Xiaoping is one of the principal architects of modern China and was an outstanding 'second Emperor'.

10.5   China's Economic Model

China's macroeconomic data has been studied in some detail in Section 3.2 of Chapter 3. The empirical study shows many remarkable results and what stands out in all the macroeconomic indicators is the comprehensive and rapid growth of China's economy.

In spite of setbacks and being constrained by a centrally planned economy, China's GDP grew steadily at the average rate of 5% in the period of 1949–1979, as shown in Figure 10.2. By 1979, as mentioned earlier, a growing population was outstripping the growth of the economy, as shown in Figure 7.2, and China needed a new paradigm to generate higher growth.

As mentioned in Section 10.3, in 1979, Deng Xiaoping together with Chen Yun made major contributions to the reforms and opening up of China. They introduced radical economic reforms by allowing for a far-reaching role for the private sector in the erstwhile centrally planned economy as well as opening up to the world and integrating China's economy with the world economy by encouraging direct foreign investments and greatly expanding international trade and finance. The reforms unlocked the potential for China's economic growth and resulted in the rapid rise of its economy, as seen in Figure 10.3.

Starting in 1978, from an economy that had a GDP one-fortieth of the GDP of the United States, China in US dollar terms is projected

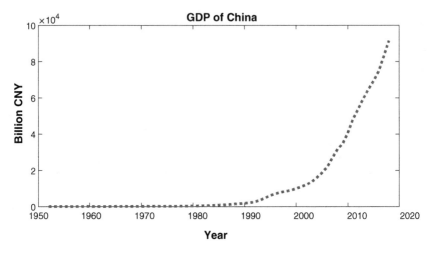

Figure 10.2.   China's historical GDP (in CNY).

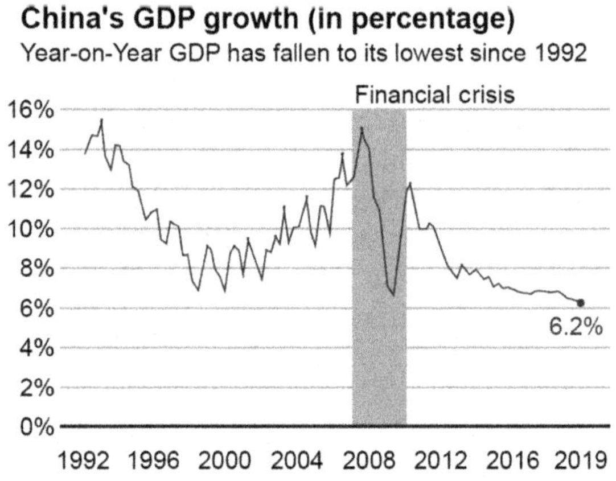

China's GDP growth (in percentage)
Year-on-Year GDP has fallen to its lowest since 1992

Figure 10.3.   China's historical GDP (in percentage).

to overtake the United States by 2026, as shown in Figure 4.3,[13] and had become the world's largest economy by 2015 in PPP terms, as shown in Figure 4.4. China's per capita GDP was comparable to that of India's in 1978 at about \$200 (1,280 yuan). In 2021, it was five times larger than that of India at \$10,000 (64,000 yuan).

Deng Xiaoping's leadership provided a new paradigm of growth for China that, with hindsight, did not weaken but instead strengthened the political power of the CPC and the socialist road chosen for China. Deng Xiaoping's analysis of the Tiananmen Square events of 1989, discussed earlier in Section 7.8 of Chapter 7, shows that, in his view, China was on the socialist road and that he was opposed to the forces that wanted to turn China into a vassal state of the West.

In sum, the radical reforms initiated in 1979 led to two pivotal changes in China's macroeconomy: one was to allow domestic private sector to coexist with the SOEs and the second was for China to economically participate and compete in the global economic system that is dominated by the developed countries. Both these steps, which tactically gave ground to domestic and foreign capital, turned out to be strategically just the opposite in that, as can be seen 40 years later, the reforms immensely strengthened China's socialist system.

10.6 Transition to a Market Economy

The transition from a centrally planned economy to a socialist market economy, also called economic liberalization, started in 1979 and was uncharted territory with China needing groundbreaking policies for making this transition. A middle class with buying power for consuming commodities produced by the private sector is required to generate an efficient market. With hindsight, launching the socialist market economy in the 1980s was an opportune time for doing so, since it was the beginning of a growing Chinese middle class.

Deng Xiaoping provided groundbreaking paradigms for accomplishing this transition. Deng Xiaoping's analysis, expressed in his article 'There is no Fundamental Contradiction Between Socialism and a Market Economy' (1985) [42], led to the creation of the socialist market economy. John Ross has provided a summary of the theoretical framework provided by Deng Xiaoping Theory for China's socialist market economy [55].

Reforms started in the agriculture with the replacement of collective farming by privately owned small-scale household farms. The next step was to maintain state ownership of large and strategic companies but to let small enterprises be privatized.

The market was used for determining the prices of privately produced 'non-strategic' goods, agricultural and light industrial products, thus contributing to the sectors' efficiency and growth. Even more important than using the market to determine prices was the devolution of political–economic power away from Beijing to the provinces and villages, allowing for local initiatives in pioneering the retooling and reorganization of Chinese society. Following the maxim of *practice is the sole criterion for testing truth*, all the initiatives and social experiments that failed were ignored and the successful ones were carried on further.

The profits and capital accumulation in the private sector were largely re-invested in light and heavy industries, thus creating a virtuous cycle of growth. The urban cost of living was kept low by subsidizing strategic goods like food, energy, transportation and other necessary goods and services, with the government's spending on subsidies being offset by reducing military expenditures.[14] The opening up of China's economy to the world further accelerated the accumulation of capital [55].

A capitalist state has two main levers for intervention in the macroeconomy: fiscal (taxation and revenue collection) and monetary (money supply, interest rates). Investments, according to economic theory, are the primary determinant in the increase of labor's productivity as well as the prime mover of economic expansion. Investments under capitalism are left in the hands of private capital [48,55]. Due to the preeminence of the PRC's state-owned industrial sector, the PRC had another key macroeconomic lever, which is direct state-funded investments in the productive economy. The state, in coordination with the reforms in agriculture and the private sector, undertook massive investments in heavy and strategic industries, infrastructure and other sectors.

The modernization of agriculture and the growth of industries have already been discussed in Section 3.1 of Chapter 3. On viewing the macroeconomic linkages between agriculture and industry, one sees that it did not happen due to pragmatic piecemeal decisions, but was based on a well-thought-out theoretical framework that provided for a close-knit economic integration and inter-locking policies for the flow of economic reforms throughout the entire economy, and, in particular, for the positive feedback between the modernization of agriculture and industrialization. Any arbitrary intervention disrupting this closely interwoven set of reforms would cause the entire process of the transition to the market economy, based on economic expansion and accumulation, to break down. In particular, if the Tiananmen Square turmoil in 1989 had resulted in the disruption of the governance of China, the transition to a market economy could have been derailed; one can even speculate that China's rise could have been thwarted.

10.6.1 *Dual-Pricing System*

The initial stage of the transition to a market economy in China was very chaotic and disruptive since the policies required had to be innovated and invented by trial and error. The fixed pricing model of the centrally planned economy did not reflect the actual market prices of commodities. For determining the market price of commodities as well as letting the private sector and the market grow, in 1984, the Chinese Government took a crucial step by introducing a two-track or dual-pricing system [46]. This system was finalized in February 1985 and entailed the following: the state would purchase a quota of commodities from private enterprises at a fixed price and enterprises exceeding their quota could sell the excess at the market price. This system went through many iterations, with the quota for state purchases and the list of commodities changing with time [50].

It becomes clear if one compares it with the disastrous Shock Therapy in Russia, discussed in Section 10.7, that, using dual pricing, allowed for a gradual and smooth transition to a market economy [51].

The dual-pricing system for determining the prices of commodities had many advantages as well as disadvantages [50]. A few of the advantages of the two-track system were the following:

- In 1984, about 80% of the total economic output was procured at government fixed prices, with the remaining amount being traded in the market. The amount with fixed prices was gradually brought down and the dual pricing system was finally abolished in 1989, with the market determining all prices.
- The dual-pricing system allowed the government to benefit from predictable fixed prices while allowing the market to slowly bring the entire pricing of commodities in line with market prices.
- It controlled inflation by providing food and subsistence to the people at affordable prices.
- It gave incentive to enterprises to produce beyond the quota for the state.

- It gave rise to a more efficient utilization of resources and good management.
- There was a compromise between central planning and market forces.
- It provided protection for domestic industries since they were assured a floor price by the state.

The major disadvantages of the two-track dual-pricing system were the following:

- It gave room for systemic corruption, since one could buy goods at state-controlled prices and then sell it at higher prices on the (black) market.
- Enterprises dishonestly hid their production output to have a lower quota for the state.
- Since the state's quota was based on past performance, the more efficient enterprises tended to be at a disadvantage.
- There was a non-optimal utilization of resources due to the state's intervention.

Recall that private enterprises were first allowed only in 1980. The following steps were taken from 1984 onward to allow the private sector and the market to grow [46]:

1. Government-fixed price controls were removed in 1989 to allow the market to determine prices.
2. The Town and Village Enterprises (TVEs), discussed earlier in Section 3.6.1 of Chapter 3 in the context of rural–urban migration, were established in 1984 and based in the rural areas. They were small, collectively owned and market-oriented enterprises, which leveraged on existing social capital to attain a high degree of efficiency and competitiveness. The remuneration of the workers was tied to their performance [22].
3. By the time they were phased out around 2000, the TVEs employed 127 million workers, had industrial value added of $227 billion, accounted for 47% of total industrial output and attained a rate of growth of 19% in the period of 1988–1999.[15]
4. Land was not privatized and the TVEs leased land from the government, with the focus of the TVEs being on remuneration based on competitiveness. The politically controversial and disruptive issues linked to land privatization were avoided.

5. The circulation of commodities was reformed with state monopoly on purchasing agricultural and other goods being gradually moved from the dual pricing to market prices. Rationing system for farm and manufactured consumer products was gradually removed by 1989.
6. Banking system was reformed to allow easy accessibility to working capital and short-term loans to the private and public sectors.
7. Private firms were allowed to issue stocks and participate in the capital markets.
8. Tax system was reformed to allow SOEs to keep part of their profit.
9. In 1994, Zhu Rongji, the Premier of China, reformed the banking system and major tax reforms were instituted, which greatly enhanced the revenue collected by the central government. The central government's revenue more than doubled from the previous year, and Beijing's share of total fiscal revenue soared to 56% from 22%, while its share of expenditures increased by only 2%.[16]

10.7 Soviet Union and China: Market Economy

The transition to a market economy is chaotic and complicated, as discussed in Section 10.6. To understand the challenges and pitfalls that China faced in economic liberalization and making a transition from a centrally planned economy to a market economy, one needs to compare it with other countries who faced and attempted a similar transition. A comparison is made between the steps taken by the CPC from 1979 onward and apparently similar steps taken by the Soviet Party from 1986 onward to see the vast difference between these two approaches. The comparison shows that the dismantling of a centrally planned economy in the manner that it was carried out by the Soviet Party ended in the collapse of the Soviet economy, whereas it was a sterling success in China.

Based on the experience of how China's reforms were carried out, one can conclude that the leadership of CPSU did not understand the relation between economic and political liberalization in dismantling a centrally planned economy. Instead of completing the economic transition, Mikhail Gorbachev, the leader of Soviet Union, introduced political liberalization that created more chaos in this transition. The Global North also used political liberalization to weaken Soviet power, and finally, all these factors led to the collapse of the Soviet Union.

Compared with the disastrous road taken by the Soviet Union, China's transition from a centrally planned economy to a socialist market economy was a resounding success. Dismantling a centrally planned economy is a complex and multi-dimensional economic and political undertaking with many interconnected issues that need to be addressed. The case of the Soviet economy shows the key and pivotal role that Deng Xiaoping played in providing China with a theoretical framework and robust and pragmatic policies for making the transition smooth and orderly.

Why did China succeed and Soviet Union fail in adopting a dynamic economic model in lieu of a centrally planned economy? The answer lies partly in the Soviet Party's economic policies. The centrally planned economy has its strong points, as discussed in Ref. [1], and served its purpose quite well during the early years of the Soviet Union. However, the centralization of the economy as well as the bias toward the military–industrial complex and heavy industry led to an acute shortage of consumer goods.[17] Decades of a centrally planned economy that had outlived its usefulness finally resulted in a failed economy, with the CPSU becoming a Party alienated from the people and with the top leadership consisting of self-serving corrupt bureaucrats.

The Soviet economy's negative factors accumulated over time and, in effect, it had become a form of bureaucratic capitalism by the 1980s. Mikhail Gorbachev's economic and political reforms, starting in 1986, took the wrong path by blindly following the policies of whole-scale privatization and market deregulation — policies that were coming from the West — and resulted in acute shortage of essential commodities, runaway inflation, pauperization of the people and ended in economic and social disasters [1]. In response, the sclerotic bureaucracy was unable to offer any other road and, in the end, tried to do an unsuccessful coup to stay in power.

The CPC, on the other hand, due to the nature of how it gained power from a bottom-up protracted armed struggle, as discussed in Chapter 7, did not lose its mooring with the people after gaining power in 1949. China had competent and seasoned leaders like Deng Xiaoping, who had the trust of the people and could institute major changes that positively affected the lives of millions of people. The CPC could also rise to the challenge of radically changing itself and engage in self-reform when confronted with the failure of the centrally planned economy.

10.8   China's Five Year Plans: An Economic Paradigm

Attempts prior to 1979 to industrialize China were only partially successful since they followed the Soviet model and relied heavily on centralized planning. The other extreme of letting the market completely take over the economy can be seen, from the repeated crisis of the developed countries, to lead to anarchy in the economy, which is specially inimical for developing countries trying to industrialize. The socialist market economy fruitfully combines the advantages of centralized planning with that of the market forces.

A major economic paradigm is China's Five Year Plans, which brings into play centralized planning and is one of the key features of the socialist macroeconomy. A bedrock of China's mixed economy is the Five Year Plans, with the current one being the 14th Five Year Plan (2021–2025). The Five Year Plans chart out directions for the socialist market economy, providing targets, guidance and leadership to both the state and private sectors of the economy.

The concept of the Five Year Plan was adopted from the Soviet Union, but China has made many innovations and improvements. The Five Year Plans are based on both top-down planning as well as bottom-up feedback from the grassroots, and incorporation of the private sector together with the SOEs. By including the private sector in the Five Year Plans, the Five Year Plans combine the *visible hand* of the government with the *invisible hand* of the market.

In addition to the Five Year Plans, there are also long-term targets that are based on the strategic goals of the CPC-PRC:

- 'Made in China 2025', a 10-year national plan announced in 2015, designed to turn China from a manufacturing giant into a global high-tech industrial powerhouse;
- complete the socialist modernization of China by 2035;
- achieve the second centennial goal of building China into 'a great modern socialist country in all respects' by 2049.

The first centennial goal has been attained in 2021 by removing absolute poverty and making China a 'moderately prosperous society in all respects'.

The long-term targets and strategic planning compliment the goals that are set down in the Five Year Plans, with both the public and private sectors operating within the strategic framework and the Five Year Plans.

10.9   China: Socialist Market Economy

In 1993, the CPC Central Committee approved the decision to establish a socialist market economic system.[18] Political power is in the hands of the CPC and private capital is not allowed to have any political influence or control over the governance of China. The key features of a socialist market economy, discussed in detail in Ref. [1], are the following:

- Chinese economy is a combination of a centrally planned economy with a market economy and constitutes what is called a socialist market economy.
- Common prosperity and balanced economic growth constitute the primary goal of the economy.
- The 'invisible hand' of the market is complemented by the 'visible' hand of the state.
- Centralized planning and private capital are complementary drivers of the economy. No monopolies are allowed in the private sector.
- Strategic industries are state owned. SOEs and private capital are equally powerful.
- The market plays a key role in price discovery and resource allocation; market is supervised to forbid abuse, especially by tech giants.
- The urbanization of the rural population is taken as the first step in the modernization of the economy.
- The market has regulations and laws for ensuring protection of both consumers and producers. In particular, regulations forbid the abuse of the market, especially by giant private companies.
- Science and technology are the primary source of productivity gains.
- Innovation and start-up enterprises are the key drivers of the economy's expansion.

Historical development of China has shown that for a socialist market economy to be successful, sovereignty and a competent and honest leadership, determining the country's policies, are necessary conditions.

Endnotes

[1] http://www.stat.go.jp/english/data/handbook/pdf/2019all.pdf.

[2] https://tradingeconomics.com/japan/interest-rate.

[3] http://www.stat.go.jp/english/data/handbook/pdf/2019all.pdf.

[4] https://www.piie.com/research/piie-charts/us-china-trade-war-tariffs-date-chart.

[5] http://www.xinhuanet.com/english/northamerica/2021-06/17/c_1310013575 htm.

[6] https://enapp.globaltimes.cn/article/1251862.

[7] http://en.qstheory.cn/2020-08/11/c_607578.htm.

[8] A more elaborate discussion on the concept of the 'national bourgeosie' and private capital is given in https://www.qiaocollective.com/en/articles/war-on-china.

[9] https://news.cgtn.com/news/3d4d544f7a556a4d/share_p.html.

[10] https://www.globaltimes.cn/page/202210/1277702.shtml.

[11] Figure 10.1 taken from: https://www.learningfromchina.net/why-common-prosperity-is-good-for-socialism-and-for-chinas-economy/#_edn4.

[12] https://news.cgtn.com/news/2019-09-15/Chinese-private-enterprises-past-present-\and-future-K0C4lsbm0w/index.html.

[13] https://www.cnbc.com/2021/02/01/new-chart-shows-china-gdp-could-overtake-us-sooner-as-covid-took-its-toll.html.

[14] https://news.cgtn.com/news/3d3d514f7a6b444f32457a6333566d54/index.html.

[15] https://www.sem.tsinghua.edu.cn/_local/9/D2/1B/79F23D539C575834E\3115 49D178_BFBDD5B2_2245AA.pdf?e=.pdf.

[16] https://rhg.com/research/chinas-fiscal-and-tax-reforms-a-critical-move-on-the-chessboard/.

[17] https://www.rt.com/news/568672-china-and-soviet-collapse/.

[18] https://www.globaltimes.cn/page/202210/1277119.shtml.

Chapter 11

Common Prosperity and Balanced Economic Growth

11.1 Introduction

With hindsight, owing to the low level of China's economy in 1979, the strategy of high economic growth was deemed necessary by China's leadership from 1979 to 2019. Furthermore, it is only when China's economy had reached a high level of strength — for its financial and manufacturing base and for its supply chains — could a new economic strategy be put into place.

A study by Piketty in 2019 on China's increasing income and wealth gap showed that the top 10% was reported to have earned 41% of the national income in 2015, up from 27% in the late 1970s. Meanwhile, the share of the national income of the population with a lower income dropped to nearly 15%, down from about 27% in 1978 [53].[1] (Lower-income entails daily spending between $10 and $50.[2])

A demand from the people, especially the younger generation, is for more equitable economic growth, a growth that does not leave anyone behind, based on a more even distribution of the results of economic growth. An equitable distribution of the country's wealth and benefits has been termed as *common prosperity*.

In 1985, at the very beginning of the current economic boom, Deng Xiaoping stated that the final objective of economic reforms, and of some people getting rich first, was to move toward common prosperity: *To take the road to socialism is to realize common prosperity step by step. Our plan is as follows: where conditions permit, some areas may develop faster than others; those that develop faster can help promote the progress of those that lag behind, until all become prosperous* [42].

11.2   Common Prosperity: Fundamental Paradigm

The CPC changed, in 2019, its earlier strategy of 'economic growth at any cost' to one seeking common prosperity based on a more balanced and high-quality growth. In particular, addressing the widening income gap due to rapid economic growth had become a major issue by the time Xi Jinping became the Party leader in 2012.

In 2020, the objective of attaining common prosperity was stated by Xi Jinping.[3] In 2021, Xi Jinping stated: *Ending poverty, improving people's well-being and realizing* **common prosperity** *are the essential requirements of socialism.*[4]

Xi Jinping once again emphasized the continuing importance of common prosperity in 2021 and further explained the concept of common prosperity: *the need for efforts to promote* **common prosperity** *in the pursuit of high-quality development and coordinate work on forestalling major financial risks. Rather than being egalitarian or having only a few people prosper, common prosperity refers to affluence shared by everyone, both in material and cultural terms, and shall be advanced step by step.*[5]

The aim and objective of common prosperity is to reduce the gap between the higher- and lower-income groups, between urban and rural population and is not targeted at expropriating the rich. Instead, the resources of the state as well as of private capital are to be used for growing those sectors of the economy that are required for achieving common prosperity. A major example of the state's role in common prosperity is the complete eradication of extreme poverty in China.

In 2012, Xi Jinping had set the target of bringing out of poverty the remaining 99 million people who were still living in extreme poverty: mostly in 832 impoverished counties and 128,000 villages. In 2020, in spite of the Covid pandemic, he declared a complete victory of removing poverty in all of China — something unprecedented in the history of China. To accomplish this task, over a period of eight years, a vast sum of $246 billion was allocated, with over 3 million public sector officials being sent to the impoverished villages; more than 1,800 people died fighting poverty on the frontlines.[6] To have an international perspective on this achievement, note that in a 40-year period (1980–2020) 70% of the world's poverty was in China. By 2020, this poverty was removed by China — 10 years ahead of the goal set by the United Nations.[7]

High-quality development requires a high-caliber workforce. Only by increasing urban and rural income can the quality of human capital be raised, resulting in gains in productivity, and thus providing the means for meeting people's spiritual and cultural needs. Common prosperity is not only about the economic well being and living standards of the people but also linked to the socialist basis of China. An uncontrolled and widening social inequality goes against the principles of socialism and would lead to the loss of support and legitimacy of the CPC. Common prosperity is the basis of long-term social solidarity and political stability and plays a key role in China's rise.

China has charted out a three-stage approach to achieving common prosperity: (a) In the first stage, from 2021 to 2025, major steps have to be taken to narrow the gap between people's income and consumption. (b) By 2035, substantial progress needs to be made, in particular by ensuring equal access to public services. (c) In line with the second centennial goal, by 2049, the gap between people's income and consumption should be narrowed to a socially acceptable level [52].

The following guidelines have been set for achieving the goal of common prosperity: (a) People need to pursue prosperity through hard work and innovation. (b) Both public and private sector should play an inter-locking and active role in promoting common prosperity. (c) A fair system of distribution of benefits from economic growth should be adopted. (d) Progress needs to be made gradually. The most difficult and challenging task is to achieve common rural prosperity [52]. A goal has been set for promoting common prosperity among farmers and, in rural areas, consolidating and expanding achievements in poverty elimination as well as advancing rural vitalization on all fronts.[8]

Noteworthy 11.1. Common prosperity, egalitarianism and consumption

There is a view that considers common prosperity to be a zero-sum game, with wealth taken from the rich and redistributed to the lower-income group. This criticism of common prosperity was expressed as follows by financier George Soros: '*Common Prosperity' program... seeks to reduce inequality by distributing the wealth of the rich to the general population. That does not augur well for foreign investors.*[9] This line of reasoning is incorrect, since as quoted earlier, Xi Jinping specifically stated that common prosperity is neither egalitarian nor favors the few: *Rather than being egalitarian or having only a few people prosperous, common prosperity refers to affluence shared by everyone.*[10] The paradigm of common prosperity redirects the economy to grow in specific sectors and allows for the full participation of private capital in these sectors. A robust industrial sector is the foundation of China's economic growth. International investors are not likely to be taken in by Soros' reasoning that common prosperity is inimical to economic prosperity. This is the reason that foreign investments continue to be drawn to China in unprecedented quantities, well surpassing foreign investments flowing into the United States.

John Ross has given an explanation of the drive for common prosperity. The author rejects the fundamental contention of many critics that common prosperity will negatively affect the economic rate of growth; he shows, using macroeconomic data from 1974 to 2019, that greater inequality in the United States led to lower economic rate of growth; on the other hand, the reduction of poverty in China has led to higher economic growth.[11]

John Ross' explanation of common prosperity hinges on the following fact: In the primary stages of socialism, the workers and

(Continued)

Noteworthy 11.1. (*Continued*)

farmers earn income by selling either their labor or the product of their labor. In contrast, the capitalists earn their income on account of their ownership of property and of capital. The profit accruing to the capitalist can either be reinvested into productive investments or be withdrawn from the productive economy in two ways: (a) luxury and superfluous consumption since this is non-productive consumption and (b) by investing profit in the paper economy and creating huge bond and stock market speculative bubbles, booms, busts and financial meltdowns [55].

Restricting wasteful and superfluous consumption of (luxury) goods by making it socially unacceptable seems to be a remote possibility. One of the biggest market for international branded luxury goods is China, and both the upper and middle classes are its biggest consumers. China accounts for 35% of global spending on luxury goods and is predicted to become the biggest global luxury market by 2025.[12] The view that superfluous consumption is undesirable was reflected in the criticism of Alibaba's Singles' Day shopping on 11-11-2021 by a Chinese newspaper, which stated: *The 'worship of turnover' is not only unsustainable in terms of digital growth but is also inextricably linked to chaos.* The article's author further states that tech giants should not expend their efforts on producing for (superfluous) consumption, which can be left to the mom-and-pop stores, but instead should strive for higher goals.[13]

11.3 Common Prosperity and Private Sector

The removal of absolute poverty in 2021 was a milestone in achieving common prosperity. China is treading a fine line between *on the one hand* avoiding the trap of egalitarianism, where hard work gets sidelined by entitlement and people seeking handouts, and *on the other hand* letting the rich get all the gains from economic growth.

One of the pillars of common prosperity is to increase the wages (income) of the working people, which is to be partly achieved by the redistribution of profits of private capital and taxing it — as well as by private capital voluntarily contributing to common prosperity. This not only raises the living standards of the working people but also creates a larger market for robust industrial production due to increased consumption by the people. Tax reforms, a welfare system and a wealth redistribution system are being instituted so that China can pursue greater equality while ensuring the continuation of economic growth.[14]

Complementing the measures taken by the state to achieve common prosperity, private capital is expected to play its due role by operating legally, paying taxes honestly, fulfilling its social responsibilities and protecting the legitimate rights and interests of both workers and consumers. In addition, private capital is encouraged to make voluntary contributions to common prosperity and hence cement its role in the country's economic development. Responding to the call by Xi Jinping for private corporations and wealthy individuals to give back to society and contribute to common prosperity, private firms made major commitments in 2021. The internet companies are playing a leading role in boosting employment, poverty alleviation and rural revitalization, with Tencent, Alibaba and JD being ranked the top three in terms of their contributions to boosting common prosperity.[15]

- Alibaba Group Holding, the world's largest e-commerce platform, said it will set aside 100 billion yuan ($15.5 billion) toward promoting common prosperity and this is to be disbursed before 2025. Alibaba's employment system provided income for more than 69 million people in 2019.
- Tencent Holdings, Asia's most valuable company by market capitalization, earmarked $7.7 billion in August 2021 for common prosperity, following a similar pledge made earlier in March 2021.
- E-commerce giant Pinduoduo launched a 10 billion yuan ($1.5 billion) fund to help lower-income rural families.
- To support common prosperity, carmaker Geely is giving out a total of 1.67 million company shares to a select 10,884 workers.

- Online marketplace JD.com announced in January 2022 that it will allocate more than \$62 million to increase welfare subsidies for more than 200,000 frontline employees.
- The Meituan platform, as of August 2020, has provided jobs and income growth for a total of 9.31 million delivery workers.
- WeChat provided income opportunities to 36.84 million in 2020. WeChat's platform network covers 1.225 billion users and 50 million merchants, and has more than 60,000 service providers who rely on WeChat Pay.

The drive for common prosperity comes at a time when income disparities are increasing and the wealth of billionaires is rising rapidly. In CPC's view, achieving common prosperity is a long-term goal. Attaining it is going to be a strenuous and complex task to be implemented in a step-by-step and progressive manner, with local authorities adopting policies to suit local conditions.[16]

11.4   Balanced 'Green' Economic Growth

The negative side effects of China's economic growth, discussed in Ref. [1], is just the tip of the iceberg and came in for repeated criticism, especially for ignoring major factors like profiteering, corruption, low wages, bad working conditions, income inequality and the damage to the environment. (Corrective measures to many of the malpractices mentioned above were taken in 2021 and are discussed in Ref. [1]). In the earlier stage, the expansion of the economy was to be achieved at any cost, in particular, paying little or no attention to the following:

- excesses of private enterprises;
- increasing wealth and income gap;
- employment and working conditions;
- using clean energy;
- protecting the environment;
- fighting rampant corruption.

Lax regulations and letting private capital have a free hand — to maximize rate of economic growth — were brought to an end in 2019 by a change of economic strategy. The CPC made a major self-correction by accepting the shortcomings of the strategy of high economic rate of growth overriding all other considerations. By 2019, the Chinese economy had matured and gained enough comprehensive strength, as shown in Chapter 3, to go to the next level of development, based on a new strategy for a more equitable and sustainable economic development.

Responding to the criticisms and leveraging on the robust and comprehensive strength of China's manufacturing and supply chains, in 2020, China announced a *change of economic strategy*, aiming for a more clean, green and equitable growth. The new paradigm of *balanced economic growth* entails a more equitable distribution of wealth between entrepreneurs and workers, curtailing the excesses of private capital, and with domestic consumption being the main driver of economic growth.

The revised paradigm for economic development is based on a number of changes in the earlier policies.

Balanced economic growth is based on promoting social fairness and justice and on the optimum relationship between efficiency and fairness, making basic institutional arrangements on income distribution, expanding the size of the middle-income group, increasing the earnings for the low-income groups, adjusting excessive incomes and prohibiting illicit income.

China has emphasized the importance of advancing balanced, coordinated and inclusive development, while stressing the need to improve the socialist market economy, strengthen balanced development among regions and promote coordinated development across industries. Basic public services are being made more equally accessible by increasing inclusive human resource investments and improving the systems of elderly care, medical security and housing supply.

The drive for a balanced growth aims at facilitating a well-regulated and healthy development of different types of capital by protecting property rights, intellectual property rights and ensuring that making money is possible only through legal means. To achieve a more equitable society, China is slowing down privatization in public services, including medical care, care for the elderly and education. It is creating new policies for raising taxes on high-income groups and capital returns. The target is to curb excessive wealth, have a system of distribution for sharing of wealth by society at large, expand the middle class and increase the earnings of the lower-income groups.[17]

By 2020, the radical change in China's paradigm for economic growth was expressed by Li Keqiang, the Premier of China, as follows: *We need to seek a balance between growth, income, and employment, and we cannot pursue economic growth based on high energy consumption and heavy pollution.*[18]

One of the main points made by Li Keqiang was to take the creation of employment as the first priority of the economy and expand the channels for employment. About 7.81 million jobs were created, from January to August 2020, and with the target of over nine million urban jobs for the year, mostly higher-quality employment for college graduates as well as enabling new entrepreneurs to flourish. Emphasis was also placed on enhancing vocational training.[19]

11.4.1   *The Environment*

Improving the environment, curbing pollution and ensuring clean cities, clean villages, clean rivers, clean air and clean oceans form a task made all the more difficult by the breakneck growth of China's economy over the last 40 years that caused heavy pollution. Reflecting the realization that a clean environment is crucial for China's future, Xi Jinping stated the following: *We want both GDP and green GDP*, and what has become a maxim in China, *Lucid waters and lush mountains are invaluable assets.*[20]

The topic of preserving and cleaning up the environment is a vast subject, full of technical questions that are addressed by the environmental sciences. China is a leading nation in green technology. For example, in 2022, 80% of all solar panels and 60% of all solar power on the grid were made in China; China generated 80% of global hydro and wind power and 70% of all electric batteries.[21]

The following are a few of the plans being undertaken by China for attaining environment-friendly growth.

Cutting back on coal-fired power generation and switching to hydropower, nuclear power and gas-fired electric generation, encouraging electric cars and so on are some of the steps that China has taken. China made nearly half of the world's total new renewable energy investment in 2017, which was a whopping sum of $279.8 billion.[22] The gradual transformation of coal power generators also resulted in an 86% reduction in sulphur dioxide emissions, 89% reduction in nitrogen oxides, and 85% less smoke dust from 2012 to 2017. Among China's 337 cities, 46.6% of the cities numbering 157 had met the air quality standard in 2019.[23]

In 2019, China invested $83.4 billion in clean energy research and development, while the US invested $55.5 billion — China's investment in clean energy research and development in 2019 was more than the total investment of the United States, Japan and India. China's total installed renewable energy capacity in 2020 was 895 GW, the largest in the world. In 2019, China contributed 4.7 million jobs in the renewable energy sector, representing 39% of the entire renewable energy employment worldwide.[24]

By 2030, China plans to establish a modern and environmentally friendly infrastructure. A few of the targets are new sewage treatment capacity of 20 million cubic meters per day, construction of 80,000 km of new and renovated sewage collection pipelines, and reclaimed water of 15 million cubic meters per day. The safe disposal of urban sludge is set to reach 90% by 2025 and the disposal and incineration of urban domestic waste is expected to reach about 1.5 million tons per day.[25]

Major cities like Beijing and Shanghai used to have low visibility due to haze and polluted air. One of the results of controlling air pollution is that these cities now have visible blue skies for most of the year. In 2021, the number of blue-sky days in Beijing came in at 288 days, or 78.9% of the calendar year, up by 112 days in 2013. In 2021, 335 Chinese cities enjoyed, on the average, good air quality for 88% of the days.[26]

Endnotes

[1]https://www.rt.com/business/532364-china-curbs-excessive-incomes/.
[2]https://chinapower.csis.org/china-middle-class/.
[3]http://www.xinhuanet.com/english/2020-11/03/c_139488141.htm.
[4]http://www.xinhuanet.com/english/2021-02/26/c_139767705.htm.

[5] http://www.xinhuanet.com/english/2021-08/18/c_1310133051.htm.
[6] http://www.xinhuanet.com/english/2021-02/26/c_139767705.htm.
[7] https://www.globaltimes.cn/page/202111/1238370.shtml.
[8] http://www.xinhuanet.com/english/2021-08/18/c_1310133051.htm.
[9] https://www.wsj.com/articles/blackrock-larry-fink-china-hkex-sse-authoritaria
nism-xi-jinping-term-limits-human-rights-ant-didi-global-national-security-
11630938728
[10] http://www.xinhuanet.com/english/2021-08/18/c_1310133051.htm.
[11] https://www.globaltimes.cn/page/202110/1236918.shtml?id=11.
[12] https://jingdaily.com/china-population-halve-luxury-hit/.
[13] https://newspursued.com/business/chinese-state-newspaper-blasts-worship-of-
turnover-after-alibabas-singles-day/.
[14] https://news.cgtn.com/news/2021-09-08/-Common-prosperity-requires-contin
ued-support-for-private-sector-13oqC7eGQBa/index.html.
[15] https://enapp.globaltimes.cn/article/1250153; https://enapp.globaltimes.cn/
article/1268039.
[16] http://www.xinhuanet.com/english/2021-08/18/c_1310133051.htm.
[17] https://www.globaltimes.cn/page/202108/1231872.shtml.
[18] https://news.cgtn.com/news/2021-03-23/Premier-China-s-loose-GDP-target-
makes-room-for-quality-growth-YRctOTTL2g/index.html.
[19] https://news.cgtn.com/news/2020-10-10/China-to-boost-employment-with-
multi-pronged-measures-Ut5aNsEZAQ/index.html.
[20] http://www.xinhuanet.com/english/2021-06/04/c_139989249.htm.
[21] https://enapp.globaltimes.cn/article/1272375.
[22] http://www.china.org.cn/opinion/2019-03/12/content_74561701.htm.
[23] https://www.globaltimes.cn/page/202006/1190346.shtml.
[24] https://news.cgtn.com/news/2021-11-09/Are-the-2-largest-economies-pulling-
their-weight-in-renewable-energy--153cGcjRux2/index.html.
[25] https://enapp.globaltimes.cn/article/1251889.
[26] https://enapp.globaltimes.cn/article/1268427; https://www.globaltimes.cn/
page/202208/1272130.shtml.

Chapter 12

Summary of Part IV

The rise of the CPC led to the establishment of the People's Republic of China (PRC) in 1949, a party-state founded as a socialist society, with the working class playing the leading role in state power. The party-state is based on the fusion of the CPC with the State, with the CPC providing the political superstructure for leadership, governance and supervision of the organs of PRC's state power. The sovereignty of the PRC and the political power of the CPC are the foundations of the different strategic choices made for China's development; without these two preconditions, it is highly unlikely that China's rise could have taken place.

The dynamism and ability to adjust and change its policies is one of the hallmarks of the CPC, which has been essential in making China's rise possible. This dynamism has been reflected in the constant changes and new paradigms that the CPC has instituted at each stage of the economy's growth.

Starting with a centrally planned economy, a major change was made, starting in 1979, to institute the socialist market economy. As the economy developed, new targets were set, such as transforming China from an industrial giant to a technological powerhouse by 2025. Growing inequalities and disorderly growth led to the crackdown on private capital and to the paradigm of common prosperity and of a green and balanced economic growth. Faced with headwinds both internationally and domestically, the concept of the dual circulation economy was introduced to weather these storms.

The socialist market economy has been instituted by the CPC for the purpose of using the advantages of both a centrally planned economy and public ownership as well as of a market economy and private capital. Properly controlling and regulating private capital, as discussed in some detail in Ref. [1], has led to the development and strengthening of the mixed economy. Far from weakening the state-owned enterprises (SOEs) and the state sector, the socialist market economy has led to the public sector becoming more powerful and continuing to be the mainstay of China's economy.

The CPC has strengthened and fortified its governance of China by undertaking economic policies that led to an unparalleled economic boom. This has enabled the CPC to proceed toward its goal of unleashing the productive power of the people, eliminating poverty and to approach, by stages, its centennial goal of transforming China into a great modern socialist country. The CPC has, since 2012, changed its development paradigm from emphasizing economic growth to that of attaining common prosperity for all.

Deng Xiaoping's groundbreaking understanding of the socialist market economy, in particular of the role of the market and private capital, provided the framework for China's economic rise. His policies and numerous practical directives in successfully managing the complex transition from a centrally planned economy to the socialist market economy were essential in changing the paradigm for China's economy, which brought into play the innovative and entrepreneurial abilities of the Chinese people and unleashed their productive energy. His view that science and technology are the primary productive force laid the foundation for China to scale the heights of innovation and high technology. The sterling results of his policies and leadership have been instrumental in China's rise. For these and other reasons, one can conclude that *Deng Xiaoping is the greatest economist of the 20th century.*

China has successfully transformed a peasant economy, with a population of over one billion people, into an industrial powerhouse in just over seven decades, with the process going through many twists and turns. The last four decades have demonstrated the pivotal role played by the leadership of the CPC in constantly reforming its policies and adapting to new developments so as to facilitate the meteoric rise of modern China. The social transformation of China has brought about historically unprecedented prosperity and upliftment of the Chinese people as well as established China as the largest engine of growth for the global economy.

Part V

Paradigms and China's Rise

Chapter 13

China's Rise

A vast and open-ended subject such as the rise of China needs many points of view. The approach taken in this book has been, as far as possible, to look at the achievements of China from an empirical and factual point of view and provide some explanations of the various policies and strategies taken by the CPC.

The purpose of this closing chapter is to try and take a long view on China's rise. Based on the plethora of details that have been discussed in the different chapters, one can also and try and see what practical lessons can other countries derive from China's experience and what theoretical and empirical principles can be abstracted about economics and governance from China's rise.

13.1   Overview of China's Rise

The last 100 years have been momentous for China. It has risen from being a fragmented semi-colonial nation and a semi-feudal society based on an impoverished, backward peasant economy to its present-day status of an advanced industrial powerhouse and one of the leading countries of the world. The analysis and facts discussed in the various chapters show that the transformation of China has no parallel in human history.

So, what is the explanation for China's ascension? It is a truism that, in the long run, the people of a country determine its destiny. However, the people are powerless to improve their lot if the country's leaders fail the people. The Chinese nation has 5,000 years of history with many achievements. However, for the entire period of feudalism (and semi-feudalism), which only ended in 1949 with the establishment of the People's Republic of China, the people at large were enslaved by the system of feudalism.

The unification of China in 1949, together with the anti-feudal revolution, established China as a sovereign and independent country, free from all foreign domination, and broke centuries old shackles of feudal subjugation of the Chinese peasantry. *The foundation of China's rise is the establishment of sovereign PRC in 1949 that brought about the liberation of the Chinese people: an epoch-making event.* This epoch-making event was achieved under the leadership of Mao Zedong.

Many countries of the world have become independent, but do not have full sovereignty to decide their future course of action, as discussed in Section 10.1 of Chapter 10. The Korean War in 1950 and the Sino-Soviet split in 1962 were both reflections of China exercising its sovereignty, even though at a high price. China's national sovereignty is an indispensable foundation for China's rise. It is the basis of China's modernization that is the result of groundbreaking paradigms and a pioneering path taken by no other nation. The pole star guiding China's socialist modernization — unlike that of the Global North — is that of creating common prosperity.

It is for this and other reasons that the *single most important factor* — and the key to understanding China's rise — is that the CPC carried out the Chinese revolution and established a sovereign China in 1949. The subsequent socialist construction was carried out from 1949 to 1979, as discussed in Chapter 7 and summarized in Section 7.10 of Chapter 7. These steps in turn laid the foundation for China's rapid rise from 1979 to 2019, as discussed in some detail in this book.

The primary goal and political *objective* of China's revolutionary wars (1927–1949) was freeing the country from foreign domination and liberating the people from feudalism. To attain this objective, the motivation and subjective enthusiasm of the CPC leaders, cadres as well as of the people was crucial to make the sacrifices and bear the hardships of a protracted people's war. One of the mistakes made by the Cultural Revolution (1966–1976) was continuing to emphasize — after the founding of the PRC — the subjective factor and mistaking politics, rather than economics, as being the key link for powering the continuing rise of China.

In 1979, China changed the *foundation* of its guiding paradigm to socialist modernization being the country's primary objective. This change — and all the policies and opening up that followed — was pivotal to China's rise. The CPC could manage to shift away from subjective thinking and dogmatism dominating China's governance by *changing its philosophical outlook* to one that is empirically grounded on 'seeking truth from facts and that practice is the sole criterion for testing truth' — an outlook that called for the implementation of policies and regulations which are successful in practice and yield tangible results.

Probably the main reason that the CPC could make fundamental changes to the very foundations of PRC's governance, starting in 1979, was that many veteran revolutionaries of the older generation, including quite a few who took part in the Long March, were still in good health and in positions of leadership. These leaders, with Deng Xiaoping being their chief representative, had the reputation and trust of the Party, of the PLA and of the people to make the drastic changes. It is doubtful that these changes could have been made by the new generation of leaders. A similar observation was made by Deng Xiaoping in the suppression of the Tiananmen Square turmoil in 1989, as discussed in Section 7.8 of Chapter 7 [42].

The primary reason for the continuing vitality of the CPC is its ability to re-invent and self-correct itself and hence provide ongoing effective governance and strategic planning, fueling China's rise. The vitality of the CPC was emphasized by Xi Jinping on the occasion of the CPC's centennial commemoration in 2021, and he made the following observation: *Today, a hundred years on from its founding, the Communist Party of China is still in its prime, and remains as determined as ever to achieve lasting greatness for the Chinese nation* [20]. There are many aspects to the role that has been, and is being played, by the CPC, as discussed in the previous chapters. Some of these are summarized in the following sections.

13.2   Summarizing China's Rise

The PRC has consolidated its political and economic system over the last seven decades and the CPC has made many innovations in its manner of governance. This has led to the success of its chosen path of development, and it can be safely surmised that China is entering a new stage of the country's rise, with many positive forces coming together to bring about a high tide of socio-economic development.

The rise of China is *unlike* the rise of other developed countries, which was largely based on colonization, slave trade and the expropriation of the gold and silver of the Americas [11,15]. The founding of PRC was the result of an anti-imperialist and anti-feudal revolution (1921–1949) carried out by the CPC. Three successive historical events paved the way for China's rise: (a) unification, (b) the initial capital required for industrialization was raised domestically by expropriating land and historically accumulated agricultural wealth and (c) instituting pro-people development paradigms.

As framed by the CPC, the anti-imperialist and anti-feudal revolution was unprecedented in Chinese history and brought about people's liberation, and in particular, freed hundreds of millions of Chinese peasantry from thousands of years of feudal bondage, feudal autocracy and feudal absolutism. Thirty years after the founding of the PRC, in 1979, China opened up to the world economy, instituted economic reforms and embarked on socialist modernization. This new economic paradigm allowed for a growing private sector complementing the state-owned sector and thus unleashing powerful productive forces, including the individual initiative of millions of entrepreneurs.

China's primary development paradigm consists of the *political* fusion of the CPC with the governance of PRC, resulting in the CPC-PRC party-state. The *economic* paradigm of combining the state sector with private enterprise has given rise to the socialist market economy, which is based on the invisible hand of the market working in tandem with the visible hand of the state.

The development paradigms organize the entire social system, both the economic base and the political superstructure, into a formidable and coherent construct. The coherence and synthesis of the base and superstructure are achieved by the overarching leadership of the CPC, which provides strategic planning and regulatory frameworks. The development paradigms have ushered in and unleashed tremendous social productive forces leading to China's meteoric rise.

The self-declared goal of socialism is to eliminate exploitation and inequality, to liberate the productive forces, to develop productivity, and this is the path chosen by the CPC to reach the goal of common prosperity and beyond. A stringent measure of CPC's performance is the degree to which common prosperity is realized.

13.3   China's Groundbreaking Paradigms

Many of the innovative paradigms employed for China's development have been reviewed and discussed in a variety of contexts in the different chapters. The underlying unifying theme of all the paradigms is to develop China into a great modern socialist country. The topics of the book were chosen to follow the logic of the paradigms that form the foundations of China's rise.

The paradigms for China's development have laid the foundation for the future continuing prosperity and stability of China. CPC's development paradigms are not just some projects on the drawing board or hypothetical and conjectural ideas, but instead are the basis of real and concrete plans and policies that have been implemented with remarkable success, and that too on a gigantic scale.

The evidence that CPC's system of governance is efficient and superior to many other countries is provided by the rapid rise of China. To contextualize the discussion on the governing paradigms of China, some of the macroeconomic indicators of China's rise — reviewed in Section 3.10 — illustrate how these paradigms have been immensely successful in ushering in China's rise to becoming an industrial giant and a global powerhouse. It is with this track record of achievements that the discussion of China's development paradigms is framed.

The paradigms that powered China's rise are summarized as follows:

- The CPC could successfully combine its Marxist ideology with China's national traditions, leading to the concept of socialism with Chinese characteristics. Xi Jinping stated: *The history of the CPC has been a process of constantly advancing the adaptation of Marxism to the Chinese context, and of constantly promoting theoretical innovation and creation.*[1]

- The philosophical principle of seeking truth from facts and that practice is the sole criterion for testing truth has freed China's planners and strategists from rigid dogmas, allowing for flexible governance and a results-based framework for assessing all policies.
- The governance of the PRC is based on the paradigm of the CPC establishing a single-party CPC-PRC state.
- The CPC provides the *political superstructure* that oversees and manages the country's bureaucracy and army as well as plays a supervisory and controlling role in China's macroeconomy,[2] including the far-flung provinces of China.
- The *principle paradigm* of China's economic model is the socialist market economy, which is a mixed economy that combines a market-driven decentralized private sector with a state sector that is under the Party's centralized control.
- China's opening up of its economy to the global economy in 1979 and allowing private capital and the market in the domestic economy led to a huge inflow of direct foreign investments and export-driven industrialization.
- China made massive investments in infrastructure and created comprehensive supply chains.
- Major investments in education and the large-scale transformation of farmers into industrial workers raised the productivity of labor.
- The CPC has charted out economic policies, such as joining the WTO, without compromising China's sovereignty. More recently, it has responded to the trade war — started by the United States in 2018 — without compromising its sovereignty.
- A country of 1.4 billion cannot be ruled without the people's participation, and the long tradition of China's peasant uprisings is a major check on the CPC's legitimacy.
- China's rise was accompanied by corruption of officials in collusion with corrupt private capital and often at the expense of the environment and the common good. Whether it was avoidable or not is still being debated.
- Efforts toward controlling and preventing rampant corruption were undertaken in earnest starting in 2013 and have largely restored the reputation of the CPC and increased people's support for the CPC: a precondition for providing effective leadership to the PRC. This is discussed in some detail in Ref. [1].

- The centralized leadership sets the strategic goals for the country that unifies and provides coherence to the country's myriad activities.
- The CPC lets market forces have full play at the local level, thus providing maximum scope for innovation and initiative of both the private entrepreneurs as well as of the grassroot Party organizations.
- China's rise required the strong centralized power of the CPC since otherwise, for a vast country like China, giving initiative to the local level could result in the center losing control, thus leading to warlordism, regionalism and separatism, and also resulting in the possible fragmentation of the country.
- Strategic planning is synchronized with a market economy and provides for greater efficiency and has an advantage compared to an economy based solely on the market.
- Private capital has played a dynamic and important role in China's rise and has pioneered many technological breakthroughs and innovations.
- The regulatory framework of the private sector includes laws forbidding the disorderly expansion of capital and forestalling the emergence of monopolies. This has been aimed at ensuring that private capital, and big tech companies in particular, serve the goal of common prosperity and that profit maximization is not at the expense of the well being of the people.
- The private sector does not hold political power in the PRC and neither does it control or influence the regulatory framework for the functioning of private capital.
- The paradigm for the optimal allocation of capital and resources is primarily based on the market. Both the invisible hand of the market and the visible hand of the state are employed for channeling and focusing investments to different sectors.
- The socialist market economy combines strategic planning with market forces. These are complementary aspects of the macroeconomy that are inseparable and in synergy. Planning is strategy and the market is tactics, with the two working together.
- Ongoing reforms of the macroeconomy are made to facilitate scientific and technological innovation as the driving force of the economy. The SMEs are provided with investments on favorable terms

compared to the big established firms so as to level the playing field.

- The paradigm of a dual-circulation economy couples domestic and international production, circulation and consumption, with emphasis on domestic circulation and consumption.
- A socialist economy is efficient for managing advanced problems like technological innovation, pandemic control, climate change, digital economy and so on because it can mobilize and regulate the entire macroeconomy.
- A major change of paradigm was made in 2019 to move from high growth rate to a green and balanced economy, with the purpose of attaining common prosperity.
- Historical bottlenecks faced by the CPC illustrate its self-corrective mechanism. The paradigm of ongoing self-supervision and self-correction of the CPC is the key to its ability to meet new, as well as ongoing, internal and external challenges.
- Sharing the prosperity of a rising China with its neighbors, and the world at large, is a major paradigm of the PRC. The Belt and Road Initiative (BRI) is an expression of the paradigm of shared prosperity.

Endnotes

[1]http://en.qstheory.cn/2021-09/08/c_657826.htm.
[2]This political superstructure was missing in China's feudal dynasties.

Chapter 14

Epilogue

The rise of China is a fast-evolving, developing and changing story. The foundations of China's rise are among the enduring factors determining the manner and direction that China takes for its future course. One of the objectives of this book is to provide a framework for understanding China's rise that, in all likelihood, is going to be one of the most important geopolitical and geostrategic events of the 21st century.

The CPC has synthesized the guiding principles of Marxism with Chinese society's social and historical foundations, giving rise to something distinctive: socialism with Chinese characteristics. This rather unique and potent fusion of two distinct and deep currents, one historical and the other contemporary, largely explains the rapidity of China's ascent as well as the fact that a modern, socialist and powerful China is restoring its place as a thriving and flourishing component of human civilization. China has charted out a unique, groundbreaking and pioneering path for its rise. To accomplish its rise, China has brought into play innovative paradigms for development that are derived from its overarching framework of socialism with Chinese characteristics.

The rise of China is an event unprecedented in human history since it has transformed itself from a backward peasant economy in 1949 to a vast industrial powerhouse, which is set to cross the critical bottleneck of the 'middle nation trap' and become a high-income country. It is poised to be one of the leaders, from the 21st century onward, of the world's scientific and technological future and to be an engine of growth for the global economy. China's rise has laid the foundation for becoming an advanced socialist society that will equal, or maybe even surpass, the existing leading nations. Many social and economic indicators show that the PRC will most likely be a long-lasting 'Red Dynasty'.

The narrative in this book has focused primarily on the internal dynamics and forces at work in China, referring to external events only when necessary, such as the role played by globalization in China's rise. All of the external forces could not have brought about this rise if not for China's domestic historical, social and political forces that were at the foundation of China's ascension. The facts, figures and analysis of this book largely substantiate this view.

The CPC has found the 'magical' key for China to amass vast amounts of wealth, and the greatest domestic challenge it faces is to maintain an incorruptible and competent leadership in the face of this immense wealth. The CPC seems to be aware of this and has demonstrated its determination to control corruption; but only history can tell how successful it will be.

The meteoric growth of China has unsettled the Global North since China's rise has the potential of comprehensively changing the existing world order that at present primarily serves the interests of the Global North. The impact of China that is of highest concern in the corridors of power in the West goes beyond economic competition. It is China's radically different social and economic system, a system which delivers sterling results, that is posing a challenge which the West has never previously faced.

Most of the countries of the world, including those of the Global North, are seeking ways for peacefully coexisting with China. The United States, however, is choosing the path of containment and confrontation, and this is the biggest challenge that the CPC–PRC is facing. It would be the wisest course of action for the world at large, as well as for the United States, if it partakes and benefits from China's rise. The containment, confrontation, decoupling and repelling of China by the United States would bring instabilities to the world that could slow down, but most likely cannot stop, the rise of China.

The developing countries are weighing the manner in which they can benefit from China's development and to what extent they can adopt a win–win strategy with respect to a powerful China. An open question is to what extent a powerful China would reshape the current global order that is currently dominated by the Global North. A great power like China can be a major force in creating a multi-polar world that benefits all countries of the world, instead of the present world order that primarily benefits only a small group of countries.

China faces great challenges to its continuing rise, both domestically and internationally [1]. With great power comes great responsibility: how China faces its challenges and whether China continues on its socialist path or turns into a hegemonic superpower is most likely going to be one of the defining factors of the 21st century global order. China is already one of the leading powers of the world, and the historical task of consolidating the position of China as a major international power seems to have fallen largely on the current generation of CPC's leaders.

To continue its rise, China has no choice but to face the storm clouds that have appeared on its horizon. China needs to achieve the hitherto unprecedented goal of developing an international strategic framework for sustaining its rise and consolidating its position as a leading global power. If the 'Red Dynasty' can succeed in this historical task, then in all probability, the PRC will be a long-lasting dynasty.

The synthesis and combination of China's rising economy and social system with the global economy and with the international political superstructure are still at an early stage. One can expect many new social innovations and technological marvels to emerge from China's ongoing modernization and integration with the world at large. The vastness and depth of China's population, size, history, economy and of its social system are China's great advantages. A powerful socialist China, having a win–win approach toward the global community of nations, has the potential of being a positive force in bringing about the historical development of humankind to a completely new and higher stage of human civilization.

References

[1] Belal Ehsan Baaquie, *Contemporary China: Socialist Market Economy and Private Capital* (To be published) (2024).

[2] Belal Ehsan Baaquie and Wang Qing-hai, Chinese dynasties and modern China: Unification and fragmentation. *China and the World: Ancient and Modern Silk Road*, Vol. 1, No. 1, 1–43 (2018).

[3] Belal Ehsan Baaquie, Bertrand Roehner and Wang Qing-hai, Bangladesh: Southern branch of the silk road. *China and the World*, Vol. 1, No. 3, 1–10, 1850019 (2019).

[4] Belal Ehsan Baaquie, Peter Richmond, Bertrand M. Roehner and Wang Qing-hai, The future of US–China relations: A scientific investigation. *China and the World*, Vol. 02, No. 01, 1950008 (2019).

[5] G. Roberts, *Why China Leads the World*. Oreil Media (2020).

[6] D. Acemoglu and J. A. Robinson, *Why Nations Fail: The Origins of Power, Prosperity, and Poverty*. Profile Books Ltd (2012).

[7] G. Kerr, *A Short History of China*. Pocket Essentials (2013).

[8] Li Wenli1 and Liu Qiang, Chinese higher education finance: Changes over time and perspectives to the future. *Procedia — Social and Behavioral Sciences* (Elsevier Ltd), Vol. 77, 388–411 (2013).

[9] Wei-wei Zhang, *The China Wave: Rise of a Civilizational State*. World Century (2012).

[10] M. Jacques, *When China Rules the World*. Penguin (2012).

[11] Yi Wen, The making of an economic superpower–unlocking China's secret of rapid industrialization, https://research.stlouisfed.org/wp/more/2015-006.

[12] G. Allison, *Destined for War: Can America and China Escape Thucydides' Trap?* Scribe Publications (2019).

[13] K. Brown, *The Future of UK-China Relations*. Blackwell (2019).

[14] 70 years in review: Chinese people's progress, https://news.cgtn.com/news/2019-09-27/China-issues-white-paper-on-China-and-world-in-new-era-Kk2Nk6ja2k/index.html.

[15] Yan, Xuetong, *Leadership and the Rise of Great Powers*. Princeton University Press (2019).

[16] K. Mahbubani, *Has China Won?* Public Affairs (2020).

[17] J. A. Goldstone, The coming Chinese collapse. *Foreign Policy*, No. 99, 35–53 (1995).

[18] G. G. Chang, *The Coming Collapse of China*. Random House (2001).

[19] Xi Jinping, *The Governance of China*, Vols. 1, 2, 3, 4. Shanghai Press (2020).

[20] Xi Jinping, Speech at a ceremony marking the centenary of the Communist Party of China, July 1, 2021, https://news.cgtn.com/news/2021-07-01/Full-Text-Speech-by-Xi-Jinping-at-gathering-marking-CPC-s-centenary-11xEAN3GOrK/index.html.

[21] Xin-zhu J. Chen, China and the US trade embargo, 1950-1972. *American Association of Chinese Studies*, Vol. 13, No. 2, 169–186 (2006), October 2006, https://www.jstor.org/stable/44288827.

[22] Li Sun, *Rural Urban Migration and Policy Intervention in China*. Palgrave MacMillan (2019).

[23] M. Perelman, *The Invention of Capitalism: Classical Political Economy and the Secret History of Primitive Accumulation*. Duke University Press (2000).

[24] K. E. Brødsgaard and K. Rutten, *From Accelerated Accumulation to Socialist Market Economy in China*. Brill (2017).

[25] F. Cost and S. Widrick, Emerging global markets: A five-country comparative study (2017), scholarworks.rit.edu/cgi/viewcontent.cgi?referer=&httpsredir=1&article\=1009&context=books.

[26] McKinsey and Company, China and the world: Inside the dynamics of a changing relationship (2019), https://www.mckinsey.com/~/media/mckinsey/featured%20insights/china/china%20and%20the%20world%20inside%20the%20dynamics%20of%20a%20changing%20relationship/mgi-china-and-the-world-full-report-feb-2020-en.pdf.

[27] L. de Mello, *Growth and Sustainability in Brazil, China, India, Indonesia and South Africa*. Organisation for Economic Co-operation and Development (OECD) (2010).

[28] Justin Yifu Lin, China and the global economy (2011), https://www.tandfonline.com/doi/abs/10.1080/17538963.2011.609612.

[29] D. Twitchett *et al. The Cambridge History of China*, Vol. 1, 3, 5–15. London: Cambridge University Press (1978–2009).

[30] F. Fukuyama, *The Origins of Political Order: From Prehuman Times to the French Revolution*. New York: Farrar, Straus and Giroux (2011).

[31] F. Fukuyama, *The End of History and the Last Man*. Free Press (1992).

[32] Mao Zedong, *The Chinese Revolution and the Chinese Communist Party* (1939), https://www.marxists.org/reference/archive/mao/selected-works/volume-2/mswv2_23.htm.

[33] G. Sima, *The Zizhi Tongjian Translated by Bo Yang*. Taipei: Yuan-Liou Publishing Co. (1993).

[34] H. H. Lai, The life span of unified regimes in China. *China Review*, Vol. 2, No. 2, 93–124 (2002).

[35] R. Dalio, *Principles for Dealing with the Changing World Order*, 1st edn. Simon & Schuster (2021).

[36] Mao Zedong, *On Practice* (1937), https://www.marxists.org/reference/archive/mao/selected-works/volume-1/mswv1_16.htm.

[37] Resolution on certain questions in the history of our Party since the founding of the People's Republic of China. Adopted by the Sixth Plenary Session of the Eleventh Central Committee of the Communist Party of China on June 27, 1981, https://www.marxists.org/subject/china/documents/cpc/history/01.htm.

[38] Resolution on certain questions in the history of our Party since the founding of the People's Republic of China (1981), https://www.marxists.org/subject/china/documents/cpc/history/01.htm.

[39] J. Ball, Did Mao really kill millions in the great leap forward? (2006), https://monthlyreview.org/commentary/did-mao-really-kill-millions-in-the-great-leap-forward.

[40] M. Kelly, Looking back at Tiananmen Square (2009), https://www.marxists.org/history/erol/ncm-7/tianamen.pdf.

[41] https://www.qiaocollective.com/en/education/tiananmenreadinglist.

[42] Deng Xiaoping, *Selected Works*, Vol. III (1982–1992). Beijing: Foreign Languages Press.

[43] S. L. Richman, *The Reagan Record on Trade: Rhetoric vs. Reality* (1988), https://www.cato.org/sites/cato.org/files/pubs/pdf/pa107.pdf.

[44] D. A. Bell, *The China Model: Political Meritocracy and the Limits of Democracy*. Princeton University Press (2016).

[45] Structure of China's Communist Party: Party cells, decision-making process, concentration of power, https://www.scmp.com/news/china/politics/article/3132921\/how-chinas-communist-party-structured.

[46] Osman Suliman, *China's Transition to a Socialist Market Economy*. Praeger (1998).

[47] Karen Jingrong Lin, Xiaoyan Lu, Junsheng Zhang and Ying Zheng, State-owned enterprises in China: A review of 40 years of research and practice. *China Journal of Accounting Research*, Vol. 13, 31–55 (2020).

[48] M. Hudson, *Killing the Host: How Financial Parasites and Debt Bondage Destroy the Global Economy*. ISLET (2015); *Stanford Law Review* (China), Vol. 65, No. 4, 697–759 (2013), April 2013.

[49] Baichun Zhang, Jiuchun Zhang and Fand Yao, Technology transfer from the Soviet Union to the People's Republic of China (1949–1966). *Comparative Technology Transfer and Society*, Vol. 4, No. 2, 105–171 (2006), August 2006.

[50] Wu Jinglian and Zhao Renwei, The dual pricing system in China's industry. *Journal of Comparative Economics*, Vol. 11, Issue 3 (1987), September 1987.

[51] M. I. Goldman, *The Piratization of Russia: Russian Reform Goes Awry*. Routledge (2003).

[52] Xi Jinping, *The Governance of China IV*. Foreign Languages Press (2022).

[53] T. Piketty, *Capital and Ideology*. Harvard University Press (2020).

[54] Li Xuran, Jack Ma is not the problem (2021), https://www.qiaocolle ctive.com/en/articles/jack-ma-is-not-the-problem.

[55] J. Ross, *China's Great Road*. Praxis Press (2021).

[56] Borge Bakken and Jasmine Wang, The changing forms of corruption in China, https://link.springer.com/content/pdf/10.1007/s10611-02 1-09952-3.pdf.

[57] F. Fukuyama, *Political Order and Political Decay: From the Industrial Revolution to the Globalization of Democracy*. Farrar, Straus and Giroux (2014).

Index

Printed in the United States
by Baker & Taylor Publisher Services